Traditional French Cooking

Jennie Reekie

St. Martin's Press
New York

Copyright © Jennie Reekie 1975

All rights reserved. For information, write:

St. Martin's Press
175 Fifth Ave.
New York, N.Y. 10010

Manufactured in the United States of America

Library of Congress Catalog Card Number: 75-40804

Library of Congress Cataloging in Publication Data

Reekie, Jennie, 1946-
 Traditional French cooking.

 Includes index.
 1. Cookery, French. I. Title.
TX719.R378 1975b   641.5'944   75-40804

Contents

A word to American readers **6**

Introduction **7**

Ingredients **19**

Soups 25

Sauces 45

Cold hors d'oeuvres and salads 55

Eggs, cheese dishes and savoury flans 73

Pâtés, terrines and galantines 95

Fish and shellfish 109

Meat 131

Poultry and game 169

Vegetables 189

Desserts 201

Breads, pastries and gâteaux 223

Index **245**

A Word to American Readers

This book was originally written for the British market and you will find occasional British terms on these pages. However, my American editor and I have gone through the book very carefully and British culinary expressions remain only where they are fully clear to American readers.

Obviously some of the fish which are readily obtainable in the United Kingdom are difficult, if not impossible, to obtain in the United States and in these cases alternative fish have been given. The way in which meat, in particular pork and bacon, is butchered is also different, so again we have given the nearest comparative cut.

Foreign cooking can be difficult and exasperating if you find the recipes complicated and ingredients unobtainable, so I have deliberately kept the recipes simple and straightforward, and few of them require ingredients which are difficult to find. I therefore hope that you will find the recipes easy to follow and be able to produce genuine French food in your own home to the delight of your family and friends.

Introduction

There are basically three different kinds of French cookery: the *haute cuisine* of the top-class chefs, made famous by such men as Escoffier, Brillat-Savarin and Pellaprat; the simpler bourgeois cooking which you will find in most bistros, cafes and in private homes, and the peasant dishes which have been passed on from generation to generation. Apart from a few exceptions, the recipes in this book are from the last two categories as most of the *haute cuisine* recipes require elaborate preparations, the mixing of two, three or sometimes even more, complicated sauces and a great deal of last-minute attention which is not really practical in this day and age.

Having said that, this does not mean that the recipes given here are only suitable for everyday cooking, and I hope that readers will find plenty of dishes suitable for serving when entertaining, as well as for good family fare. However, in view of the rising cost of food, I have kept to a minimum recipes which use lobsters, crayfish, oysters, beef fillet, truffles and similar expensive ingredients.

France is the largest country in Western Europe and it is therefore not surprising that its cooking varies enormously, not only from north to south and east to west, but also from province to province. Each of these, although overlapping in some respects, has its own definite identity and for this reason I have written a little bit about most of them and the food both produced and eaten there which I hope you will find interesting.

Orléanais

Whilst it is not really logical to start describing the provinces of France with what, to many people, may be an obscure province somewhere in the middle of northern France, it is this area of France which I know best. When I was thirteen my parents decided my rather poor French needed helping along and I went to spend my summer holidays with a family who live just south of Orléans on the edge of the Sologne. I wish I could say that it was here that I first learnt to appreciate French food, but it really would not be true. I think, being garrulous by nature, I was concerned far more with learning French so that I could talk to everyone, than thinking about the food. The point, however, which has stuck firmly in my mind is the trouble they went to, not only to cook the food but also to buy it. Instead of buying their milk from the local grocer or dairy, all the children had to take it in turns to ride their bicycles (none of which had any brakes, as I recall) three miles to the farm, with the milk churns hanging over the handlebars. We used to buy the butter straight from the dairy, where it was cut off from large slabs according to how much was required, and enormous quantities of bread were of course bought daily from the village.

The Sologne is one of the biggest and most popular hunting areas of France. The woods and moorland are full of pheasant, wild duck, partridge, snipe, woodcock, rabbit and hare, and there are still quite a number of wild boars. Driving back from the *son et lumière* at Blois a few years ago my husband was rather alarmed to see one running along the road beside the car. Fortunately it headed back into the wood and did not dash across the road in front of us, as I fear that we and the car would probably have suffered more than it if we had collided!

In the latter part of the twentieth century, Orléans, '*la cité de* Jeanne d'Arc', is probably better known for its vinegar than for its fifteenth-century heroine. Bottles of '*le véritable vinaigre d'Orléans*' can now be found in the gourmet section of some supermarkets.

Île de France

Paris has always been the centre for the great French chefs, but the *haute cuisine* has not been the only good thing to come out of this area. Ask any Frenchman and he will tell you that Paris has the best bread in the whole of France, and not only bread but delicious cakes, pastries and *gâteaux*. The old markets of Les Halles in the centre of Paris, where many prudent housewives used to shop, as well as the shopkeepers and restaurateurs, has now been replaced with a large modern market at Runjis, near Orly airport. Even so you will still find a few housewives prepared to make the journey out of Paris in the hope of finding bargains amongst the profusion of fresh meat, fruit, vegetables and cheeses which are brought here from every corner of France. Also to the south of Orly is the area where Brie cheese is made, which the Duc de Talleyrand described as the 'King of Cheeses'. Brie is a cheese which travels extremely well and a friend of mine in Fontainebleau told me that the best Brie she had ever eaten was not there, but in London! Two other cheeses which come from this region are Coulommiers, which is rather similar to Brie but not as strong, and Fountainebleau, which is a very light cream cheese.

Bretagne

Too often Normandy and Brittany are lumped together in people's minds as being the same, and whilst these two provinces do have similarities, they are also dissimilar. The seaside meadows coming in from the bay of the Mont-Saint-Michel, to the east of St Malo, produce delicately flavoured, salt-meadow lamb and mutton which is prized throughout France. Traditionally the roast leg is served with cooked white haricot beans (see page 158), which is why when a dish is described as being '*à la bretonne*' it usually means that it is accompanied by haricot beans.

As Brittany forms a peninsula, it is really not surprising that the Bretons are very good fishermen. The mackerel, herring and whiting are particularly good, but it is for shellfish that Brittany is renowned. I have myself picked excellent mussels off the rocks

THE COOKERY REGIONS
OF FRANCE

MILES 0   50   100
KILOMETRES 0   80   160

Fécamp

Le Havre

Caen

R. Seine

NORMANDIE

Chartres

BRETAGNE

Rennes

ORL

TOURAINE

Blois

Angers

Tours

R. Loire

ANJOU

Belle Ile

St Nazaire

BE

Nantes

Ile d'Yeu

Ile de Ré

La Rochelle

Ile d'Oléron

LIMOUSIN

Limoges

BAY

Périgueux

OF

PÉRIGORD

BISCAY

R. Dordogne

BORDELAIS

Bordeaux

R. Garonne

GASCOGNE

Bayonne

Toulouse

PAYS BASQUE

Oloron

BÉARN

L

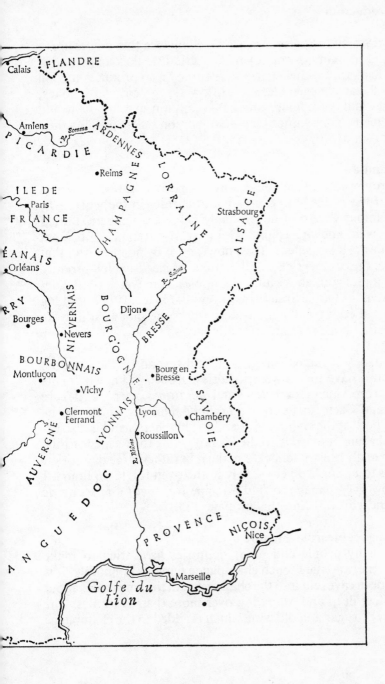

at St Brévin, near St Nazaire. Stalls selling lace-thin *crêpes* are to
be found in many of the towns and griddle cakes made out of
buckwheat are another specialty. Brittany also produces a good
crop of early vegetables, cauliflowers, greens, artichokes,
potatoes and, of course, onions — autumn in London would
hardly be the same without the Breton onion sellers pushing their
bikes around!

Normandie

The province of Normandy, with its rich pastures, produces
some of the finest butter, cream and cheeses in the world, the
most famous cheese of all probably being Camembert. But, if
not as well known, Isigny, Gournay, Neufchâtel and Pont
l'Évêque are all excellent. This, however, is by no means all that
is made; the countryside is full of apple orchards which produce
eating apples and, above all, cider apples from which both cider
and Calvados (apple brandy) are brewed. On a cliff overlooking
the sea at Fécamp is the monastery where the monks still make
Benedictine liqueur from aromatic herbs.

Normandy is famed for its fish, and several of the Norman
towns also have their own specialties. Rouen is known for its
ducks, from which superb *pâtés* and *ballottines* (see page 104) are
made, and Caen for its *tripe à la mode de Caen* which can be
bought both at the *charcuteries* and the butchers', and is also exported in cans. I toyed with the idea of giving the recipe for this,
but it is really only practical to make it in rather large quantities,
as it has to be cooked very slowly in the oven for 12-16 hours. I
did, however, manage to find a recipe for *boeuf à la mode de
Caen* and you will find this on page 135.

Champagne, Picardie, Flandre

Whilst many people and many countries have tried to make
champagne, the true French champagne remains inimitable. It is
still made in caves cut into the chalk beneath the vineyards, about
70-100 feet deep and extending over more than 125 miles. The
quantity of sugar and old wine which is added to the champagne

determines whether it will be dry or sweet, and there is one champagne which is made with no extra sugar. To come back down to earth — it is also northern France which produces most of the beer, some in this region and some in Alsace and Lorraine. Much of the land therefore is given over to the cultivation of hops and grapes, and parts of it are the most highly industrialized areas of France. Even so it still manages to boast such delicacies as Ardennes ham, Maroilles, said to be the strongest cheese in France, and *petit-gris escargots* which are canned and exported.

Alsace and Lorraine
These two provinces, which have been the subject of so many disputes and wars, have a *cuisine* almost entirely of their own — half German, half French. This is especially true of Alsace, which was under German domination for so many years and where even the names of the towns sound German — many people could be forgiven for thinking that Heiligenstein is not a town in France. Here you will find *sauerkraut*, cheesecake (see page 235) and *kugelhopf* but, despite this, it is the home of several world-famous dishes which are decidedly French; *quiche Lorraine* (see page 88) and *pâté de foie gras* (*en croûte*) of Strasbourg. Alsace is also noted for its fine wines — Riesling, Traminer and Gewürztraminer — and for its Kirsch, Framboise, Mirabelle, Poire and Quetsche liqueurs.

Savoie
As with other border provinces, the food of the Savoie bears a marked similarity to that of the neighbouring country, in this case Switzerland. With the ever-increasing number of ski resorts, this area of France has probably seen more changes in the last ten years than any other. Prior to this, it was typical of many other mountainous regions, with small villages and hill-farmers who concentrated on dairy produce. But, despite the changes, and the increased wealth they have brought to the local inhabitants, much remains the same, particularly as far as the cooking and the local produce are concerned. The Savoyard cheeses, Beaufort, Tomme, Emmenthal, Reblochon and Vacherin are to be found

in all the local shops, although you are unlikely to see many of them, apart from Reblochon and perhaps Tomme, outside France.

The *charcuterie* is good, in particular the smoked and salted sausages and hams; and the white wines are excellent. In 1735 green Chartreuse liqueur was made from the recipe for a cordial which had been invented in the sixteenth century by a courtier of Henri IV. He gave his secret formula to the monks of the order of Saint Bruno and they still make Chartreuse at Voiron, although now in a modernized distillery.

Limousin, Auvergne, Berry, Bourbonnais, Nivernais
The 'lumping together' of these five provinces is in no way intended as a slight on their *cuisine*, but each province is only small and much of the cooking in the central part is similar, although there are recipes peculiar to each province. The area is full of small streams and rivers and there are many ways of serving the trout, perch, carp, tench, pike, crayfish and salmon which are to be found in them.

In the Auvergne you will find the black *lentilles de Puy* (see page 21) and the deliciously simple, country dish of *lentilles au petit salé* (see page 165). In the Limousin they grow superb black cherries with which they make *clafoutis* (see page 215), and in the Nivernais, Charolais beef is reared which is prized by gourmets throughout the world.

Anjou and Touraine
The Loire, which rises in the Languedoc and flows through the Lyonnais, Bourgogne, the Nivernais and Berry, has become a very large river by the time it reaches the Orléanais, Touraine and Anjou and finally flows out to the Bay of Biscay past Nantes. Quite apart from the beautiful *châteaux* all along its banks, it is also a fisherman's paradise, and a number of truly delicious dishes are made from the fresh-water fish found in it. One of the most famous of these is poached pike (or other fresh-water fish) with *beurre blanc*, a sauce made from shallots, reduced white wine, wine vinegar and fresh unsalted butter (see page 47). There

is in fact some dispute between the towns of Angers and Nantes in Brittany as to which of them was the inventor of this delicacy which both claim as their own.

Tours is renowned for its superb *charcuterie*, particularly the *rillettes de porc* (see page 102), but other specialties of the surrounding area are black pudding, chitterlings and, although some readers may hate the idea, lark *pâté*. The vineyards produce some fine wines, the white semi-sparkling wine of Vouvray and the *rosé* of Anjou possibly being the best known, although the red and white wines of Saumur and Touraine are also excellent.

Périgord
Think of the Périgord and one word will probably immediately spring to mind — truffles. Despite the fact that these fungi have been prized for so many years, attempts to cultivate them have always failed, and the only way of finding them still remains to take a dog (usually a highly intelligent mongrel) or a pig to sniff them out for you. On the subject of man's inability to understand about truffles Alexandre Dumas wrote, 'The most learned men have been questioned as to the nature of this tuber, and after two thousand years of argument and discussion their answer is the same as it was on the first day: we do not know. The truffles themselves have been interrogated, and have answered simply: "eat us and praise the Lord".' The truffle season lasts from the beginning of December and continues through until March. They are generally to be found anywhere from 2-24 inches below the ground, among the roots of oak trees, but they are sometimes found near birch, elm, willow and aspen. As pigs have been used to hunt for truffles for generations, it is only logical that there is a large pig industry in the area. Much of the agricultural land is poor, so in addition to pigs, sheep and geese are kept, both of which can make use of the poor grazing. For years the local cheese was consequently made of ewes' milk and many lovers of Roquefort will be glad of this. Milk is now sent from all over France to make this cheese, but a good proportion of it is still made from the milk of the local sheep. As in Alsace, the geese are reared primarily for their liver, and the *pâté de foie gras* of the Périgord is said to equal that of Strasbourg.

Provence and Niçois

This comparatively small area of France has had an enormous amount of influence on the cooking of the entire country. The well-known Provençal ingredients of eggplants, peppers, garlic and especially olives, have all contributed to the cooking of the region, and consequently to that of the nation. Many of the indigenous dishes were in fact brought in by the Romans when they invaded in the first century BC and this is probably one of the few places where the *cuisine* of the great Roman Empire has remained, at least in part.

As the thousands of holidaymakers who pack the Côte d'Azur each summer know, there is an endless variety of fish to be bought or eaten in the restaurants from Nice round to Marseille and beyond. Many of these fish you will never see in your local markets, but red mullet, bass and other rough equivalents can all be found, especially now so much frozen fish is available.

The coastal area, however, is only a small part of Provence, and it is inland that you will find the olive groves and market gardens. The fruit and vegetable markets and shops are a delight to the eye with the rich purple, red, green and orange of the eggplants, tomatoes, peppers, grapes, figs, oranges and peaches.

Olive oil is the strongest characteristic of Provençal cookery and very little butter is used. You will find olive oil in all the great Provençal and Niçois dishes — *bouillabaisse* (see page 122), *äioli* (see page 51), *salade niçoise* (see page 63). Much of the distinctive taste of Provençal cooking also lies in the abundance of fresh herbs which grow on the hillsides and can be bought in the shops. It is on these herbs that the bees feed, and produce the Provençal honey.

As one would expect, some of the Niçois cooking is similar to that of Italy and in many of the butchers' and grocers' you will find fresh ravioli and noodles for sale.

Languedoc

The Languedoc is one of the largest provinces and although, especially in the southernmost parts, the cooking is similar to that of Provence, the people are fiercely proud of their own identity.

The two most famous dishes to come out of this area are *cassoulet* (see page 164) and *brandade de morue* (see page 111). Bordering on the Périgord, the western parts of this province also specialize in geese and pigs, and both provinces produce superb *confits d'oie* (see page 177) which is goose preserved in its own fat, and *charcuterie*, particularly the various smoked sausages and hams. This is also a great fruit-growing area, especially for soft fruit such as plums, prunes and peaches. The apricots grown on the Roussillon Plain account for nearly the entire national production.

Basque, Béarn, Bordelais and Gascogne

First and foremost, Bordeaux and the surrounding area is famous for its wines — Médoc, Graves, Entre-Deux-Mers, Sauternes and Barsac, to name but a few, and in Gascony, south-east of Bordeaux, they make Armagnac, the oldest and proudest French grape brandy. Just to the north of Bordeaux, the Dordogne and Garonne rivers join and the Gironde estuary is filled with sturgeon from which some of the finest caviar in the world is prepared.

Much of the cooking is similar to that of the Périgord. Here too the farmers' wives make their own *saucisses* and *confits d'oie*, duck and pork, and from these produce such good country fare as *garbure* (see page 30). In this area you will find that goose fat is used in the cooking where in Normandy and the north they use butter and in Provence olive oil. The geese are fed mainly on corn, which is the chief cereal crop, and the *foie gras* which is made here is said to account for 60 per cent of the total production of France. It would not be right to end an account of this area without mentioning *pipérade*, that delicious concoction of eggs, sweet peppers and onions (see page 78).

Bourgogne, Lyonnais and Bresse

Outside France these areas are better known for their wine than their food, producing both Burgundy and Beaujolais wine, but certainly within France the cooking of the Lyonnais is held high. It was a Lyonnais pastrycook who first made *quenelles de bro-*

chet (see page 129) in the first quarter of the fourteenth century. Brillat-Savarin came from the neighboring Bresse, which is where Bresse Bleu cheese and Bresse chickens come from, the latter having been described as the 'king of chickens and chicken of kings'. Many recipes which have now become almost household names originated in Burgundy — *coq au vin* (see page 172), *boeuf à la bourguignonne* (see page 135) and *fondue bourguignonne*; and here too you will find snails and frogs.

Ingredients

There are various reasons why French cooking leads the world, but ranked high among them is the wealth of natural food resources of the country, and the pride of its people in producing and cooking only the best. It is almost impossible to produce first-class food out of poor ingredients and the French housewife is painstaking with her shopping. She will quite rightly reject the bruised apple and the fatty meat which her British or American counterpart will probably begrudgingly accept. A little extra care taken when shopping can often save you hours in the kitchen, and it is worth remembering that it is sometimes better to pay a few pennies more for a piece of meat, fish or vegetables, as it may well prove cheaper in the end. In order to produce really first-class food it is also important to understand and know a little about the basic ingredients and for this reason I have written a few brief lines about some of the major ones.

Bouquet garni
This consists of a bunch of herbs, tied together and generally wrapped in a piece of muslin, which is added to soups, stews and casseroles. The classic bouquet consists of three parsley stalks, a small bay leaf and a sprig of thyme, but this can be varied by adding marjoram, winter savory, a small sage leaf, etc. In Provence they generally add a strip of dried orange peel as well. It is now possible to buy commercially made sachets of *bouquet garni* — these are not as nice as making your own with fresh herbs but are certainly better than nothing at all.

Butter
The use of butter in French cookery is important, adding extra flavour to many dishes and so I have not used margarine. However, in many of the recipes if you wish to substitute margarine, either for economy or health reasons, there is no reason why you should not. For cooking I find it is generally best to use either unsalted or lightly salted butter.

Cheese
The French generally use Emmenthal, Gruyère and Parmesan for cooking, although in certain local areas where a hard cheese is made this is also used. I have kept to the use of these three cheeses, but if for economy you should wish to substitute another suitable cheese, there is no reason why you should not.

Drippings
The fat and juices left in the pan in which meat or poultry has been cooked may be strained through cheesecloth and refrigerated for future use. In the following recipes, lard may be substituted when drippings from a roast are not available.

Garlic
Without garlic many dishes would be rather tasteless and boring, but it is important not to use so much garlic that it completely overpowers the taste of the other ingredients. Garlic also varies considerably in strength according to where it is grown and the time of year, so it is advisable to try to buy from the same source. Personally I find that the larger heads, which may be just a little bit more expensive, have a much better flavour, and larger cloves are also much less of a problem to peel. When adding garlic to a recipe it should also be remembered that if it is not cooked, e.g. if it is in a salad, you will have a much stronger garlic flavour than in a dish which is cooked slowly for a long time.

Ham
Most French ham is in fact raw or only very lightly smoked, such as Bayonne, Ardennes and Morvan hams. The most common

way of serving is sliced wafer-thin as an *hors d'oeuvre*, although the country-cured hams are also often used as a basis in soups and casseroles.

Herbs

In all the recipes, unless I have stated otherwise, I mean chopped fresh herbs. If you wish to use dried herbs, you should use a quarter of the amount recommended, as these are much stronger than fresh herbs. The increased publicity has recently made fresh herbs, which have a much better flavour, more widely available and most of the common herbs are very easy to grow. You do not need an enormous garden to have a small herb patch, and many of them will flourish in a window-box. The use of herbs is a very personal and subtle thing. The flavour of the herb should not camouflage whatever it is flavouring and many people have very definite ideas as to which herbs they prefer.

Lentils

In all the recipes in which lentils are given it is most important that you use either the greeny-brown lentils, or, if you are feeling extravagant, the black *lentilles de Puy* which have a superb flavour, stay whole during cooking and do not go to a puree as the orange lentils do. The green lentils can be found in supermarkets. The *lentilles de Puy* are rather more difficult to track down and you are unlikely to find them except in very high-class shops.

Mushrooms

The French use a wide variety of mushrooms — *cêpes, girolles*, boletus. These are not generally available outside France and, apart from country dwellers who know their edible fungi, I would not recommend anyone to start looking for them. Dried *cêpes*, which need soaking in water for some time before cooking, can be obtained from good grocers, although these are generally German ones and rather expensive. In all the recipes in this book cultivated mushrooms can be used, but where I have stipulated button mushrooms, this is generally necessary; open mushrooms, which have rather black undersides, will colour the sauce or dish and turn it into a dirty grey colour which will not look very appealing.

Mustard
There are several varieties of French mustard which vary in strength from very mild to mustards which are almost as strong as English mustard. Unless I have stated otherwise I have used a medium mustard in all these recipes.

Olive oil
Nothing compares with the flavour of olive oil and although for economy you may sometimes use corn, nut or vegetable oil, the result is unlikely to taste the same. This is particularly true of dishes in which the oil is an essential part, such as *ratatouille*, and in many salads. If, however, you do wish to economize (and with the price olive oil is now I am sure many people will), I would suggest that you buy very good-quality olive oil and mix this with a cheaper oil. If you do like using olive oil and find that you use quite a lot, it is well worth buying it in gallon cans, as you generally make quite a saving this way.

Olives
These are used extensively as a garnish, and as an ingredient in many recipes. Both green and black olives are generally pickled in brine, but here again the flavour of olives sold loose in quality grocers' and gourmet shops is much better than that of those sold in jars. If you do buy olives loose from the grocer they can be stored — preferably in the refrigerator — covered with oil, which can either be olive, corn or nut.

Pepper
Once ground the flavour of pepper rapidly deteriorates, so for this reason freshly milled pepper should always be used, if possible. There are three varieties of peppercorn: green, which is the mildest, black and white, which is the strongest. Black peppercorns are the best to use for general cookery.

Salt

If it is at all possible, I would always recommend that sea salt is used as its flavour is far superior to that of the free-running, refined table salt. Always remember before you serve any savoury dish to taste it and adjust the seasoning, as it is this final adjustment which can often make or mar a meal.

Shallots

Shallots are used extensively in French cookery, particularly that of the northern and central areas. It is said that shallots are to the Angevins what garlic is to the Provençals. If you have difficulty in obtaining shallots, you can replace them with onions, but if you have a garden you could try growing them as they are extremely easy to cultivate.

Vanilla

The use of vanilla beans is preferable to that of vanilla extract. Vanilla beans can be used again and again; after use you simply wipe them dry and store them ready for the next time. You can also make vanilla sugar by placing a vanilla bean in a jar with superfine sugar and leaving it for about a week. Every time you use some sugar from the jar all you then have to do is top it up with more sugar and shake it well.

Vinegar

Wine vinegar, either red or white, is preferred for the recipes in this book, though a good cider vinegar may also be used.

Wine

Cooking with wine is not necessarily as expensive as many people imagine. While you will probably find that if you use a glass or two of a good table wine it will add a subtle flavour to your dish, there is no reason why you should not use the cheap *vin ordinaire* which is used in all the French homes. An inexpensive domestic wine would also be a good choice. Several of the recipes only require a few tablespoons of wine and in those that require rather more you will generally find that long, slow cooking of cheap cuts of meat or poultry are involved. In this way the addition of the wine turns a humble stew into a truly delicious dish which you would be very happy to serve at a dinner party, at very little extra cost. Apart from a few exceptions the wine is always reduced, either by long, slow cooking in stews and casseroles, or by rapid boiling. This reduction is important as it is only then that the wine imparts a good mellow flavour to the food. As with other herbs, flavourings and seasonings, it is important to exercise restraint and not to 'drown' the flavour of the fish or meat with the wine.

Soups

In past years home-made soups seem to have gone out of fashion, and it was really only when I came to testing the recipes for this book that I remembered how delicious and, above all, how easy they are to make. For some reason many people seem to think that soup takes hours to make, but in fact only a very few of the soups in this chapter are cooked for longer than an hour and they do not require elaborate preparation. The French are particularly fond of vegetable puree soups and you will still find that most families start their evening meal with a bowl of soup.

In this chapter I have also given detailed recipes for making stock. Stock is another thing which many people shy away from in the belief that it takes hours and is not really worth the bother when bouillon cubes are so easy. Whilst I do find bouillon cubes invaluable, I also find that with them all my food starts tasting the same. Although stock does take a long time to cook, the initial preparation only takes about 15 minutes and you can then forget all about it for hours. Most butchers will let you have bones very cheaply and you can also use poultry and game carcasses. I find it well worth while as it keeps for a couple of weeks in a refrigerator, provided you strain it and boil it up every other day. Stock freezes well and you can either store it in plastic containers as it is, or you can reduce the stock by rapid boiling to about a quarter of its original volume. Pour this highly concentrated stock into icecube trays and freeze. When you want some stock all you then have to do is to remove one or two of the cubes and mix with water.

Fonds brun
Beef bone stock

This is a good basic stock recipe which can, of course, be adapted to suit your needs and what you have available. If you are making the stock for *consommé* (see page 27) or aspic jelly (see page 28) it is essential to enrich it by adding the shin of beef.

2 lb beef bones
¼ lb shin of beef, finely chopped (optional)
10 cups water
1 onion
1 carrot
1 small turnip
1 leek
1 *bouquet garni*
salt

Trim off any excess fat from the bones and wash them well. Put them and the beef, if used, into a saucepan with the cold water. Bring slowly to simmering point and leave uncovered for about 15 minutes, skimming off all the grey scum. Peel or clean and roughly chop all the vegetables. Add them to the pan, with the *bouquet garni*, cover and simmer very gently for 4-5 hours. During cooking, skim off any fat and scum which comes to the surface. Allow the stock to cool, then strain it and add salt to taste. Leave to become cold and skim off any fat. The stock may be frozen or stored in the refrigerator and boiled up every other day.
Makes about 1½ cups

Fonds blanc
White stock

Make as the brown stock above, but replace the beef bones with veal bones, and the chopped shin of beef with veal; omit the turnip.

Fonds de volaille ou de gibier
Chicken or game stock

Make as the brown stock (page 26), but replace the beef bones and beef with a chicken, duck, hare, pheasant or other poultry or game carcass. Omit the fresh beef and the turnip and reduce the quantity of water to 5 cups. If using uncooked bones (which will give a better stock), cook for about 2½ hours, but if using bones which have already been cooked, cook for only 1 hour.

Consommé

Consommé can either be made from good beef bone stock (see page 26) or from the stock from a *pot-au-feu* (see page 137). The flavour of the stock is all-important and, as *consommé* is quite a bother to make, before you start taste the stock and adjust the seasoning. If it is weak and insipid, finely chop about ¼ lb. of lean shin of beef and simmer the stock with this for about 1 hour.

5 cups brown stock (see page 26)
2 egg whites
2 washed egg shells, crushed
2 tablespoons sherry

Remove any fat from the stock and put into a pan with the lightly whisked egg whites and egg shells. Heat very gently, beating with a wooden spoon and bring just to boiling point. Leave for 10 minutes, during which time the whites will form a crust on the top and all the impurities will adhere to this. Turn off the heat and leave the saucepan for another 10 minutes, then either pour into a jelly bag, previously rinsed out in hot water, or into a clean tea towel or several layers of cheesecloth in a colander placed over a bowl. Leave until all the stock has dripped through the bag or cloth, leaving the sediment behind. Add the sherry to the

strained broth and either reheat gently or allow to cool, then chill if serving cold.
Serves 4

Aspic
Aspic jelly

Follow the recipe for *consomme* (see page 27), but add 4 table-spoons or 4 envelopes gelatine to the stock with the egg shells.

Potage Périgord
Périgord soup

1 slice of bread
1 small lean strip bacon
1 teaspoon chopped parsley
1 teaspoon chopped chives
½ teaspoon chopped thyme
1 small shallot, very finely chopped
2 cloves garlic, crushed
salt and freshly milled black pepper
1 egg yolk
1 large cabbage leaf
2 tablespoons butter
2 large onions
3¾ cups stock

Cut the crusts off the bread, soak the bread in a little water, then wring very dry with your hands. Cut any rind off the bacon and chop the bacon very finely. Put the bread and bacon into a small bowl with the parsley, chives, thyme, shallot, 1 clove of garlic, and seasoning. Mix well and bind with the egg yolk. Cut out the stem end of the cabbage leaf and cook the cabbage in boiling salted water for a minute. Drain and rinse in cold water. Lay the cabbage out flat, put the bacon mixture in the centre, roll up the

leaf, turning in the sides, to make a neat parcel and secure with fine string or thread. Melt the butter in a pan, add the onions and cook over a gentle heat for about 20 minutes until pale golden brown. Add the remaining clove of garlic and the stock, and bring to the boil. Add the stuffed cabbage leaf to the soup, cover and simmer gently for about 45 minutes. Remove the cabbage parcel, take off the string or thread and cut into slices. The soup is served with a few slices of the cabbage in each bowl.
Serves 4

Soupe à la savoyarde
Celeriac soup

1 small celeriac, about ¾ lb in weight
1 small potato
1 medium-sized onion
1 leek
4 tablespoons butter
3¾ cups stock
1¼ cup milk
salt and freshly milled black pepper
2 slices white bread
½ cup grated Gruyère cheese

Peel or clean the vegetables and slice them very finely. Melt the butter in a saucepan, add the vegetables, cover and cook gently for about 20 minutes, shaking the pan several times to prevent them from sticking. Add the stock, milk and seasoning and continue cooking for a further 10 minutes. Toast the bread lightly on both sides. Sprinkle with the grated cheese and grill until the cheese has just melted. Cut the bread into 1-in squares and serve them with the soup.
Serves 4-6

Garbure

This is a classic French peasant soup from the south-western provinces and is hearty enough to be a meal in itself. Generally some *confit d'oie* (see page 177) is added to the soup, but as few readers are likely to have any in their larder I have replaced this with garlic sausage.

½ lb smoked pork butt, cut in one piece
2 potatoes, peeled and thinly sliced
2 leeks, chopped
2 carrots, chopped
1 ⅓ cups fresh shelled (or use frozen) fava or broad beans
1 ⅓ cups fresh shelled (or use frozen) peas
2 teaspoons paprika
1 sprig thyme
3 cloves garlic, crushed
⅔ cup garlic sausage, chopped
7½ cups stock
salt and pepper
1 lb white cabbage, shredded
1 cup grated cheese

Cut the pork into ½-in. cubes. Put into a pan over a gentle heat until the fat runs. Add potatoes, leeks and carrots and cook gently for 5 minutes, shaking the pan frequently. Add all the remaining ingredients with the exception of the cabbage and cheese and bring to the boil. Lower the heat and simmer gently for 30 minutes, then add the cabbage and cook for a further 15 minutes. Serve the soup sprinkled with the cheese.
Serves 8

Soupe à l'ail
Garlic soup

Needless to say this recipe comes from Provence and is only for garlic addicts!

2 tablespoons olive oil
14 cloves garlic
5 cups good stock
salt and freshly milled black pepper
¼ teaspoon mace

Heat the oil in a pan and gently fry the garlic for about 8 minutes. Pour in the stock and add the salt, pepper and mace, cover the pan and simmer gently for 15 minutes. Strain the soup into a tureen and serve with crisp toast.
Serves 4

Soupe aux marrons
Chestnut soup

This is a speciality of the Bourbonnais.

½ lb chestnuts
2 tablespoons butter
2 leeks, finely chopped
1 onion, finely chopped
2 carrots, finely chopped
2 stalks celery, finely chopped
2 small white turnips, finely chopped
5 cups stock
salt and pepper

Make a small slit in the top of each chestnut. Put the chestnuts into boiling water for a minute, then peel off the shell. Melt the butter in a pan and gently cook the chestnuts, leeks, onion, carrots, celery and turnips for about 10 minutes. Pour over the stock, and bring to the boil. Cover the soup and simmer gently for about 1 hour. Taste and adjust the seasoning before serving.
Serves 6

Soupe à l'oignon
Onion soup

6 tablespoons butter
5 large onions, finely chopped
5 cups good beef stock
salt and pepper
4-6 rounds of French bread
½ cup grated Gruyère cheese

Melt the butter in a large, heavy pan. Add the onions and cook *very gently*, stirring from time to time until the onions are a pale golden brown; this will take about 45 minutes. Add the stock and seasoning, cover the pan and simmer gently for a further 20 minutes.

Toast the bread lightly on both sides, then sprinkle one side of each piece of toast with the cheese. Grill until the cheese is golden brown. Pour the soup into individual soup bowls and, just before serving, top each one with the toasted bread.
Serves 4-6

La soupe au pistou
Vegetable soup with pesto sauce

As in many other Niçois recipes, there is a strong Italian influence here; this soup is like *minestrone* with *pesto*, the famous Genoese sauce, stirred in just before serving.

⅓ cup haricot (dried white) beans
4 tablespoons olive oil
1 large onion, finely chopped
2 tomatoes, skinned and chopped
5 cups stock
¼ lb green beans
1 zucchini, chopped
2 medium-sized potatoes, peeled and diced
⅓ cup broken vermicelli
3 cloves garlic

1 tablespoon chopped basil
grated Gruyère cheese

Soak the haricot beans in cold water overnight. Drain, cover with
fresh salted water and cook for about 1½ hours until just tender.
Drain.

Heat 2 tablespoons of the oil in a large saucepan and fry the
onion gently for about 5 minutes. Add the tomatoes and cook for
a further 2 minutes. Pour in the stock and bring to the boil. Add
the green and haricot beans, zucchini and potatoes. Cover and
simmer gently for 40 minutes, then add the vermicelli and cook
for a further 10 minutes.

While the soup is cooking, pound the garlic and basil to a
paste, preferably in a pestle and mortar, then gradually add the
remaining oil, drop by drop, so that it becomes part of the paste.
Remove the soup from the heat and stir in the paste. Turn into a
soup tureen and serve with grated cheese.
Serves 4-6

Potage berrichon
Green vegetable soup

4 tablespoons butter
1 medium-sized onion, finely chopped
1 small lettuce, finely chopped
1 small green cabbage, finely chopped
⅔ cup fava or broad beans
⅔ cup peas
¼ lb green beans, cut in thin slices
5 cups stock
salt and pepper

Melt half the butter in a pan, add all the vegetables and fry
gently, without browning, for about 10 minutes. Add the stock
and seasoning. Bring to the boil, cover and simmer gently for 1
hour. Just before serving, taste and adjust the seasoning, then
stir in the remainder of the butter.
Serves 6

Potage crème d'artichauts
Cream of artichoke soup

This soup originated in Brittany and should really be made with fresh globe artichokes, but I have tried making it with 2 14-oz cans and the result was excellent. Add the chopped and drained artichoke hearts to the onions, then use the liquor from the cans with stock to make 5 cups. You may also use 2 9-oz packages of frozen artichokes, thawed.

10 large globe artichokes
4 tablespoons butter
1 medium sized onion, finely chopped
5 cups stock
salt and pepper
2 tablespoons heavy cream

Cook the artichokes in boiling water for about 40 minutes, or until you can easily pull out the leaves. Drain and leave until cool enough to handle. Take off all the leaves of the artichokes; these are not used in the soup and can be served cold with *sauce vinaigrette* or mayonnaise for another meal. Carefully remove the hairy 'choke' and discard.

Coarsely chop the artichoke hearts. Melt half the butter in a saucepan and gently fry the onion for about 2 minutes. Add the artichoke hearts, cover and cook over low heat 5 minutes. Add the stock and seasoning and bring to the boil. Cover and simmer for 20 minutes. You may put the soup in a blender and blend for a minute then strain, or you may strain the vegetables, pass them through a mouli or sieve and then return to the stock. Reheat the soup and stir in the remaining butter and the cream just before serving.
Serves 6

Soupe à la bretonne
Haricot bean soup

1⅓ cups haricot (dried white) beans
4 tablespoons butter

2 large onions, chopped
2 leeks, chopped
5 cups stock
salt and pepper

Soak the beans overnight in cold water, then drain and discard the water. Melt half the butter in a large saucepan and gently fry the onions and leeks over low heat for about 10 minutes. Add the beans, stock and seasoning, cover and simmer gently for about 2 hours, or until the beans can be crushed easily. Either put the soup into a blender and blend until smooth or pass the strained vegetables through a vegetable mouli or sieve and then mix with the stock. Reheat the soup and adjust the seasoning. Stir in the remaining butter just before serving.
Serves 6

Potage au potiron
Pumpkin soup

2 tablespoons butter
1 leek, chopped
1 medium-sized onion, chopped
1 small turnip, chopped
2 lbs pumpkin
3¾ cups stock
1 *bouquet garni*
pinch sugar
salt and pepper
⅔ cup heavy cream

Melt the butter in a pan and gently fry the leek, onion and turnip for about 10 minutes. Peel the pumpkin, remove the seeds and cut into 1-in cubes. Add to the pan with the stock and *bouquet garni*. Cover and simmer gently for 45 minutes. Remove the *bouquet garni*. Either put the soup into a blender and blend for a few minutes, or pass the strained vegetables through a sieve

or a vegetable mouli and then mix with the stock Return to the pan, add the sugar, taste and adjust seasoning. Reheat gently and add the cream just before serving.
Serves 6

Crème tourangelle
Mixed vegetable soup

⅔ cup haricot (dried white) beans
⅔ cup *flageolet* or dried baby lima beans
3 leeks, chopped
2 large onions, chopped
5 cups stock
2 tablespoons butter
4 tablespoons heavy cream

Soak the haricot and *flageolet* beans overnight in cold water. Drain and put into a saucepan with the leeks, onions and stock. Bring to the boil, cover and simmer gently for 1½-2 hours. Either put the soup into a blender and blend for 1 minute or pass the strained vegetables through a vegetable mouli or sieve, then mix with the stock. Reheat the soup, and just before serving, stir in the butter and cream.
Serves 6

Crème Dubarry
Cauliflower soup

1 small cauliflower
2 tablespoons butter
1 onion, chopped
2½ cups stock
2½ cups *sauce béchamel* (see page 45)

Break the cauliflower into small flowerets. Heat the butter in a saucepan and gently toss the onion and cauliflower in this for a

couple of minutes, then pour over the stock. Cover and simmer for about 30 minutes or until the cauliflower is very tender. With a fork, or a potato masher, lightly break up the cauliflower, then stir in the *sauce béchamel*. Heat gently together for about 5 minutes, taste and adjust the seasoning before serving.
Serves 4-6

Soupe aux lentilles
Lentil soup

1 small smoked pig's knuckle
1 cup lentils (see page 21)
1 onion, chopped
1 *bouquet garni*
5 cups water
2 tablespoons butter
⅔ cup light cream

Soak the knuckle overnight in cold water. Drain and put into a saucepan with the lentils, onion, *bouquet garni* and water. Cover and bring to the boil. Simmer gently for about 1½ hours or until the lentils are very soft. Remove the knuckle and *bouquet garni* and either put the soup into a blender and blend for a minute until smooth or pass the vegetables through a sieve or vegetable mouli and then blend with the strained stock. Finely chop the meat and add this to the lentil purée. Reheat gently, and just before serving, stir in the butter and cream. Taste and adjust seasoning, then serve.
Serves 6

Potage parmentier
Potato and onion soup

4 tablespoons butter
1½ lb potatoes, peeled and thinly sliced

2 large onions, chopped
2 cups stock
2 cups milk
salt and pepper
1 very small bay leaf
¼ teaspoon mace
1 egg yolk
4 tablespoons heavy cream
2 tablespoons chopped parsley

Melt the butter in a large pan and gently fry the potatoes and onions for about 10 minutes. Pour in the stock and milk and add the seasoning, bay leaf and mace. Cover the pan and simmer gently for 20 minutes. Either put the vegetables into a blender and blend for 1 minute or put the vegetables through a sieve or vegetable mouli, then blend with the strained stock. Turn the soup back into the saucepan and bring to the boil. Blend the egg yolk with the cream, then stir in about 4 tablespoons of the hot soup. Pour this back into the pan and heat gently, but do not allow the soup to boil. Turn into a soup tureen and sprinkle with the parsley before serving.
Serves 4-6

Soupe aux tomates
Fresh tomato soup

2 strips lean bacon, chopped
4 tablespoons butter
1 onion, chopped
1½ lb tomatoes, chopped
5 tablespoons flour
3¾ cups stock
1 teaspoon sugar
salt and pepper

Put the bacon and butter into a saucepan and cook gently for a few minutes, then add the onion and cook for a further 8 minutes

or until the onion is just golden. Add the tomatoes and cook until they are pulpy, then stir in the flour and cook for about 2 minutes. Gradually stir in the stock and bring to the boil stirring all the time. Add the sugar and seasoning, cover and simmer gently for 1 hour. Either put the soup into a blender and blend for 1 minute, then strain to remove all the skin and seeds, or put the vegetables through a sieve or vegetable mouli then mix with the strained stock. Reheat the soup gently, taste and adjust the seasoning.
Serves 4

Crème de concombres
Cream of cucumber soup

1 large cucumber
2½ cups stock
2 tablespoons butter
1 tablespoon flour
⅔ cup light cream
salt and pepper

Wash the cucumber and peel off almost all the skin. Cut into 1-in pieces and put into a saucepan with the stock. Bring to the boil, cover and simmer gently for about 20 minutes or until the cucumber is very soft. Either put the cucumber and stock into a blender and blend for 1 minute or put the cucumber through a sieve or vegetable mouli, then blend with the strained stock. Melt the butter in a saucepan, add the flour and cook for a minute. Gradually stir in the cucumber mixture and bring to the boil, stirring all the time. Cook for 3-4 minutes, then lower the heat and stir in the cream. Taste and adjust the seasoning before serving.
Serves 4

Potage cressonnière
Potato and watercress soup

2 bunches watercress
4 tablespoons butter
1 medium-sized onion, finely chopped
1 lb potatoes, peeled and sliced
2½ cups stock
2 cups milk
salt and freshly milled black pepper
¼ teaspoon mace
⅔ cup light cream

Trim off a small bunch of top leaves of the watercress for garnish. Melt the butter in a pan and fry the onion and potatoes together for about 5 minutes without browning. Add the stock, milk, seasoning and mace, cover the pan and simmer gently for about 15 minutes. Wash the remainder of the watercress and chop roughly, including the stalks. Add to the pan and cook for a further 10 minutes. Either put the soup into a blender and blend for 1 minute, or put the vegetables through a sieve or vegetable mouli, then blend with the strained stock.

This soup can be served hot or cold. If serving hot reheat the soup gently, stir in the cream and heat without boiling; if serving cold add the cream to the puréed soup and chill for 3-4 hours. Sprinkle the soup with the finely chopped, reserved watercress leaves before serving.
Serves 6

Purée aux épinards
Spinach soup

4 tablespoons butter
2 lb fresh spinach
salt
1¼ cups light cream

1¼ cups good chicken stock
freshly milled black pepper
good pinch of grated nutmeg

Melt the butter in a large saucepan, add the well-washed
spinach and salt. Cover and cook gently for about 20 minutes or
until the spinach is tender. Either put the spinach, together with
the liquid in the pan, into a blender and blend for 1 minute, or put
the spinach through a sieve or vegetable mouli, then blend with
the strained liquid. Return the puréed spinach to the pan with
cream, stock, pepper, nutmeg and salt, if necessary, and heat
gently without boiling.
Serves 4-6

Vichyssoise
Chilled leek and potato soup

3 tablespoons butter
3 leeks, chopped
2 onions, chopped
1 lb potatoes, peeled and sliced
3¾ cups chicken stock
salt and pepper
pinch of grated nutmeg
1¼ cups light cream
2 tablespoons chopped chives

Heat the butter in a pan, add the leeks and onions and cook for
about 10 minutes. Add the potatoes, stock and seasoning. Bring
to the boil, cover and simmer gently for about 45 minutes. Either
put the soup into a blender and blend for a minute or pass the
vegetables through a sieve or vegetable mouli and then mix with
the strained stock. Add the cream, taste and adjust the
seasoning, then chill for 3-4 hours. Serve the soup very cold
sprinkled with chopped chives.
Serves 4-6

Potage froid aux carottes
Iced carrot soup

2 tablespoons butter
1 lb carrots, peeled and sliced
1 large onion, chopped
1 leek, chopped
2½ cups stock
salt and pepper
1 teaspoon sugar
⅔ cup light cream
2 tablespoons chopped chives

Melt the butter in a saucepan and fry the carrots, onion and leek for about 5 minutes. Add the stock and seasoning. Cover and simmer gently for about 1 hour. Remove the pan from the heat and either put the soup into a blender and blend until smooth or pass the strained vegetables through a vegetable mouli or sieve and then mix with the stock. Add the sugar and most of the cream, taste and adjust the seasoning and then chill. Just before serving, spoon over the remaining cream to form an attractive pattern and sprinkle with chives.
Serves 4

Crème de coquillages
Cream of shellfish soup

In Brittany, where this recipe comes from, a wide variety of shellfish are used, such as scallops, oysters, mussels, whelks, cockles, but you can use any one of these. If you like, you could also use cooked prawns or shrimps. These should be shelled and the shells added to the stock used for cooking the fish.

2 lb mixed shellfish (see above)
2½ cups water
few parsley stalks
1 onion, chopped
2 tablespoons butter

4 tablespoons flour
1¼ cups white wine
⅔ cup heavy cream
2 egg yolks
2 tablespoons chopped parsley
salt and pepper

Clean the shellfish and put into a saucepan with the water, parsley stalks and onion. Cover and bring to the boil. Simmer gently for about 10 minutes or until all the fish are cooked. Strain the fish and reserve the cooking liquid. Remove all the fish from their shells.

Melt the butter in a pan, add the flour and cook for 1 minute. Remove from the heat and stir in the wine. Return to the heat and bring to the boil stirring all the time. Stir in the liquid from cooking the fish and simmer gently for 5 minutes. Blend the cream with the egg yolks and add to the pan with the fish and parsley. Heat gently without boiling for a few minutes. Taste and adjust the seasoning before serving.
Serves 6

Potage crème au crabe
Cream of crab soup

This recipe can also be used for lobster.

1 medium-sized cooked crab, about 3 lb
2½ cups water
1¼ cups white wine
peeled zest 1 lemon
juice ½ lemon
salt and pepper
1 *bouquet garni*
4 tablespoons butter
1 onion, chopped
¼ lb mushrooms, finely chopped
1¼ cups light cream
2 egg yolks

Remove all the meat from the crab. Put the well-scrubbed shell and the claws into a saucepan with the water, wine, lemon zest and juice, seasoning and *bouquet garni*. Cover and simmer for 30 minutes.

Melt the butter in another saucepan and fry the onion and mushrooms gently for 10 minutes. Add the strained crab stock and crab meat and heat gently. Blend the cream with the egg yolks and stir in about ½ cup of the hot stock, then pour it all back into the soup and heat gently without boiling. Taste and adjust the seasoning before serving.

Serves 6

Sauces

French sauces are world-renowned, so there is little need for me to extol their virtues. With one or two exceptions the sauces given here are very basic ones, but even these are important in their own way. A good *sauce de tomates* will quickly perk up a very ordinary meat loaf, or make a good starter to a meal with boiled noodles, and a couple of spoonfuls of *sauce espagnole* will vastly improve an ordinary broiled chicken.

Two sauces which are extremely simple but, in my view, extremely important, are mayonnaise and *sauce vinaigrette*. A simple green salad of lettuce with a few chopped fresh herbs and each leaf nicely coated in dressing can be superb, but if the dressing is made with poor oil or there is too much vinegar, or if it is not well seasoned, it can be quite horrible, and it is these very small points which differentiate between the mediocre and the good cook. Home-made mayonnaise is really not a great trouble to make and keeps so well in the refrigerator that I would always ask readers to make it themselves rather than using the bought varieties which cannot compare in flavour to that which you make yourself.

Sauce béchamel

1 ½ cups milk
1 small bay leaf
3 peppercorns
⅛ teaspoon mace

few parsley stalks
piece of carrot
½ onion
2 tablespoons butter
4 tablespoons flour
salt and pepper

Put the milk into a saucepan with the bay leaf, peppercorns, mace, parsley, carrot and onion. Bring slowly to the boil, cover and simmer very gently for 10 minutes, then strain. Melt the butter in a clean saucepan, add the flour and cook gently for about 2 minutes. Remove the pan from the heat and very gradually beat in the strained milk. Return the pan to the heat and bring to the boil, stirring all the time until the sauce is smooth and thick. Taste and adjust the seasoning.
Makes 1¼ cups

Sauce Mornay
Cheese sauce

1¼ cups *sauce béchamel* (see above)
½ cup grated Gruyère cheese
¼ cup grated Parmesan cheese
1 teaspoon French mustard

Heat the *sauce béchamel* in a saucepan until it is just boiling, then stir in the cheese and mustard. Cook gently, stirring all the time until the cheeses have melted.
Makes 1½ cups

Sauce Bercy
Shallot and white wine sauce

This sauce goes very well with grilled steaks and chops.

⅔ cup shallots, finely chopped
1 ¼ cups dry white wine
3 tablespoons butter
2 tablespoons chopped parsley
juice ½ lemon

Put the shallots into a saucepan with the wine. Bring to the boil and simmer gently, uncovered, for about 20 minutes. Remove the pan from the heat, add the butter and when it has melted, the parsley and lemon juice. Serve the sauce with a ladle in a sauce-boat.
Serves 4-5

Beurre blanc
Butter and shallot sauce

This sauce is traditionally served in the Loire region with pike or shad poached in a *court bouillon* (see page 109). It can, however, be served with other fresh-water or sea fish and I have found it delicious served with poached trout. Its only disadvantage is that, apart from the initial reduction of the wine and vinegar, it really does have to be made at the last minute.

3-4 shallots
3 tablespoons white wine vinegar
3 tablespoons white wine
¾ cup unsalted butter

Chop the shallots very finely and put into a small saucepan with the vinegar and wine. Put over a medium heat and cook, un-covered, until almost all the liquid has evaporated. Allow to cool.

Replace the saucepan over the lowest heat possible and stir in 2 tablespoons of the butter. When it has softened and become creamy, stir in another 2 tablespoons of the butter and continue in this way until it has all been used. The important point when making this sauce is not to let the butter become too hot and melt; it should just remain thick and creamy.
Serves 4

Sauce espagnole
Rich brown sauce

This is a particularly good sauce to use with chicken.

4 tablespoons drippings
⅓ cup bacon, roughly chopped
1 small onion, chopped
1 carrot, chopped
1 shallot, chopped
½ cup flour
2½ cups beef stock
⅓ cup mushrooms, or mushroom stalks
2 tablespoons tomato paste
2 tablespoons sherry
salt and pepper

Heat the drippings in a small, heavy saucepan. Add the bacon and fry gently for about 3 minutes, then add the onion, carrot and shallot and continue frying for about 5 minutes. Stir in the flour and cook, very gently, stirring from time to time until the flour is a golden brown. It is important for this sauce that the flour is browned, but it must on no account be burnt. Slowly stir in the stock and bring to the boil, stirring all the time. Add the mushrooms, cover the pan and simmer gently for 30 minutes. Stir in the tomato paste, sherry and seasoning, re-cover and simmer for a further 15 minutes. Strain the sauce through a sieve, pressing the vegetables well to extract as much liquid as possible. Reheat the sauce, taste and adjust the seasoning.
Makes 2½ cups

Sauce de tomates
Tomato sauce

2 tablespoons olive oil
1 clove garlic, crushed
1 onion, finely chopped

1 strip lean bacon, chopped
1½ lb tomatoes, chopped
salt and freshly milled black pepper
pinch sugar
1 teaspoon chopped fresh basil

Heat the oil in a pan and fry the garlic, onion and bacon gently for 5 minutes. Add the remaining ingredients, cover and simmer gently for 30 minutes.

Either put the sauce into a blender and blend for a minute, then pour through a sieve, or just sieve the sauce. Return to the sauce-pan, taste and adjust the seasoning and reheat gently before serving.
Serves 4-6

Sauce bigarade
Orange sauce

This orange sauce is excellent served with roast duck or with pork. It should be made with bitter Seville oranges, but as these may not be available, you can make it with ordinary oranges and omit the sugar.

2 Seville oranges
2 tablespoons drippings from the duck or pork
1 tablespoon flour
⅔ cup stock
1 tablespoon sugar
2 tablespoons port wine
salt and pepper

Using a potato peeler, peel the zest from the oranges, taking care not to take off any of the white pith. Cut the orange zest into fine strips and put into a pan of boiling water for 5 minutes, then strain.

Heat the drippings, add the flour and cook gently, stirring frequently until golden brown. Remove from the heat and gradually stir in the stock. Return to the heat and bring to the

boil, stirring all the time, and add the juice from one of the oranges, the sugar, port, orange zest and seasoning, together with any meat juices. Heat gently for 2-3 minutes.
Serves 4-6

Mayonnaise

Making mayonnaise with olive oil is very expensive and so I generally use about 3 parts corn oil (not vegetable oil) to 1 part of olive oil. It will keep for a couple of weeks in a covered container in the refrigerator, but should be put in the warmest part as if it becomes too cold it will separate. I personally think it is better stored in a screw-topped jar rather than a plastic container, as it sometimes seems to take on a rather 'plastic' taste in these. Mayonnaise can be made in a blender as well as by hand.

2 egg yolks
½ teaspoon salt
1 teaspoon French mustard
freshly milled black pepper
2 tablespoons wine vinegar
1¼ cups oil

To obtain the best results, all the ingredients should be at room temperature. You can make mayonnaise with eggs straight from the refrigerator, but there is a much greater chance of it curdling. Using either a wire whisk or wooden spoon, whichever you find easier, beat the egg yolks with the salt, mustard, pepper and 1 tablespoon of the vinegar. Then, gradually, beat in the oil drop by drop until you have added about half of it and the mixture looks thick and shiny. At this stage the oil can be added a little quicker. When all the oil has been incorporated, beat in the remaining vinegar.

If you add the oil too quickly and the mixture curdles, all is not lost. Break a fresh egg yolk into a clean bowl and beat the curdled mixture into this a teaspoon at a time.
Makes a generous 1½ cups

Aïoli
Garlic mayonnaise

Aïoli is the name of a sauce, and the name of a dish comprising cold poached fish, hard-boiled eggs and cooked vegetables (generally potatoes, carrots, green beans, etc) — all served with *aïoli* sauce. The sauce is sometimes known as the 'butter of Provence' and in some of the villages during the summer '*aïoli* feasts' are held with long trestle tables put out in the village square heaped with fish, usually salt cod, vegetables, French bread and large bowls of the golden sauce. You may not think it sounds particularly appetizing, but in fact it is excellent and makes a very good summer lunch or supper with poached fresh cod and vegetables — provided everyone likes garlic!

3-4 cloves garlic, crushed
2 egg yolks
freshly milled black pepper
pinch salt
1 ¼ cups oil, preferably olive oil

Make the sauce as you would mayonnaise (above) adding the garlic to the egg yolks, but for this sauce, you do not use any vinegar.
Makes 1¼ cups; enough for 4 people

Sauce rémoulade
Remoulade sauce

This is generally served with broiled meat or fish, but is also used in salads such as *céleri rémoulade* on page 70.

1 ¼ cups mayonnaise
2 teaspoons French mustard
2 teaspoons finely chopped capers
1 teaspoon chopped parsley
1 teaspoon chopped tarragon
1 teaspoon chopped chervil (if available, or use extra parsley)

Put the mayonnaise into a bowl, add all the ingredients and mix well. This sauce should be left for at least 30 minutes before serving for the flavours to infuse.
Makes 1¼ cups

Sauce gribiche
Herb and caper sauce

An excellent sauce to serve with cold meats in place of mayonnaise.

2 hard-boiled eggs
salt and pepper
1 teaspoon French mustard
1 tablespoon wine vinegar
1¼ cups olive oil
4 gherkins, finely chopped
1 tablespoons chopped parsley
1 teaspoon chopped tarragon
2 teaspoons chopped capers

Cut the eggs in half, take out the yolks and put them into a bowl. Pound with a wooden spoon together with salt, pepper and mustard. Very gradually beat in the oil, a drop at a time as if making mayonnaise (see page 50). When half the oil has been incorporated, beat in the vinegar, then gradually beat in the remainder of the oil. Stir in the gherkins, parsley, tarragon, capers and chopped white of egg, and adjust the seasoning.
Makes a scant 2 cups

Sauce vinaigrette
French dressing

I have suggested making a large quantity of dressing which you can store for up to 6 weeks in a cool place, then use as required. If, however, you do not want to keep the dressing, and make a smaller quantity, it will be improved by the addition of a very little finely chopped onion, chives and parsley.

2 teaspoons French mustard
½ teaspoon salt
freshly milled black pepper
1¼ cups olive oil
4-6 tablespoons wine vinegar
1 clove garlic, peeled

Put all the ingredients into a screw-topped jar or old wine bottle and shake vigorously until well blended.
Makes a scant 2 cups

Sauce hollandaise

Hollandaise sauce is generally thought of as being very difficult to make. However, it is not nearly as hard as many people imagine as long as you follow a few basic rules. Never put it over boiling water — only hot — or you will end up with scrambled eggs. Make sure the egg yolks are really thick before you start to beat in the butter and only beat in the butter a little at a time. Hollandaise sauce does not keep well and should be used as soon as possible after it is made, but you can keep it warm for a limited period, i.e. about 30 minutes if you leave it over hot water.

juice ½ lemon
1 teaspoon water
salt and pepper
3 egg yolks
½ cup softened butter

Put the lemon juice, water and seasoning into a bowl over a pan of hot, *not boiling*, water. Add the egg yolks and a small piece of butter and beat well with a whisk until the mixture is thick. Add the remaining butter to the egg yolks, a spoonful at a time, whisking well. When all the butter has been incorporated the mixture should be thick and glossy.
Makes about ¾ cup

Cold hors d'oeuvres and salads

The French, especially those of southern France, excel themselves when it comes to cold *hors d'oeuvres* and salads. I first learnt about them when I worked in the summer as an *au pair* for a family who had a house up in the mountains outside Nice. As the numbers for lunch varied each day between 12 and 24 we used simply to make salads, slice up various salamis and other *charcuterie* and lay them out on a large table with the inevitable bottles of wine and bowls of fresh olives.

In my opinion there is nothing nicer than a good salad, but nothing nastier than that piece of meat or cheese plopped on a plate with a few mangy lettuce leaves, two slices of beet, a quartered tomato and the odd slice of cucumber. There is no great art to the making of salads; it is largely a question of practice and, above all, remembering to dress and garnish them attractively. I think it is also much nicer, although a little more trouble, to make separate salads of lettuce, cucumber, tomato, etc, rather than mixing them all up in one bowl. It is also well worth while experimenting with different ingredients; legumes such as beans and lentils make really delicious salads which are particularly useful in the winter when the green vegetables tend to be very expensive and generally not of very high quality.

Salade de moules
Mussel salad

4 quarts fresh mussels
4 shallots, peeled and chopped
few parsley stalks
2 sprigs fresh thyme
1 bay leaf
freshly ground black pepper
1¼ cups water
4 tablespoons olive oil
2 tablespoons wine vinegar
2 tablespoons chopped parsley
salt

Clean and prepare the mussels as for *moules marinière* (see page 126). Put the shallots, parsley stalks, thyme, bay leaf, pepper and water into a large saucepan and bring to the boil. Add the mussels, cover with a tightly fitting lid and cook quickly, shaking the pan constantly. As soon as the mussels are all open, quickly remove from the heat. Take the mussels out of their shells and put into a bowl with the oil, vinegar and parsley. Toss the mussels lightly while still warm and season to taste with salt and pepper. Turn into a serving dish and leave until cold.
Serves 4

Salade de crabe
Crab salad

1 medium-sized crab
½ cup + 2 tablespoons mayonnaise (see page 50)
1 teaspoon strong French mustard
good pinch cayenne pepper
2 stalks celery, very finely chopped
2 green onions, finely chopped
salt and pepper
4 large lettuce leaves

Remove all the meat from the shell, body and claws of the crab. For this recipe use the green or brown meat, the white meat and any coral. Put the meat into a bowl with the mayonnaise, mustard, cayenne pepper, celery, most of the onions and seasoning. Mix well. Place a lettuce leaf on an individual plate or in a scallop shell and spoon the crab mixture on top. Sprinkle with the remaining onions.
Serves 4 as an hors d'oeuvre

Salade de boeuf
Beef salad

1 lb cooked beef
6 gherkins, very thinly sliced
1 small onion, very finely chopped
6 tablespoons *sauce vinaigrette* (see page 52)
2 tablespoons finely chopped parsley

Cut the beef into small, thin slices and put into a bowl. Add the gherkins, onion, *sauce vinaigrette* and half the parsley and mix well. Arrange on a serving dish, sprinkle with the remaining parsley and leave for at least 2 hours before serving.
Serves 4-6

Mousse à la truite fumée
Smoked trout mousse

2 large smoked trout
2 tablespoons softened butter
juice ½ lemon
1¼ cups heavy cream, lightly whipped
salt and freshly milled black pepper
pinch cayenne pepper

Skin and bone the trout. Pound the flesh with a wooden spoon in

a bowl or in a pestle and mortar. Add the softened butter and lemon juice and mix well. Fold the fish into the lightly whipped cream and season to taste with salt, black pepper and cayenne pepper. Turn into a dish and chill.
Serves 6 as an hors d'oeuvre

Anchoiade
Anchovy paste

This is a Provençal specialty; it can be eaten as a snack, and is excellent spread on small pieces of toast and served with drinks, although it will make everyone even thirstier!

1 large clove garlic
2 1¾-oz cans anchovies in olive oil
2 teaspoons lemon juice
freshly milled black pepper
4 thick slices of French bread or, if serving with drinks, use two slices of ordinary white bread, but about ⅓ in thick

Pound the garlic in a mortar, then add the anchovies together with the oil from the cans, and work to a rough paste. Stir in the lemon juice and pepper. Toast the bread on one side only and while it is still hot spread the anchovy paste on the untoasted side, pressing it well into the soft bread. Either broil under a moderate flame, or cook in a hot oven (450°F) for about 4 minutes before serving. Serve hot, and if serving with drinks, cut the toast into small squares.
Serves 4 as a snack or 8 with drinks

Citrons farcis aux sardines
Lemons stuffed with sardines

4 medium-sized lemons
1 3¾ oz can sardines in oil
4 tablespoons heavy cream

1 tablespoon chopped parsley
4 black olives, finely chopped
salt and freshly milled black pepper

Cut the tops off the lemons and dig out the pulp and juice using a knife and a small spoon. Put this on one side and cut a small slice off the base of the lemons so that they stand up. Mash the sardines with the oil from the can, and lightly whip the cream. Blend the sardines with the cream, parsley, olives and seasoning and then stir in the strained lemon juice to taste. Pile this mixture back into the lemon cases and chill for at least 1 hour. Top with the lemon caps before serving.
Serves 4

Pan bagna
Open tomato sandwich

This is a rough, peasant sandwich which is excellent for summer picnics or light lunches with a modest bottle of red wine.

1 small French loaf
1 clove garlic
3 tablespoons olive oil
4 tomatoes
1 green pepper
1 1¾-oz can anchovies in olive oil
a few capers
a few olives

Cut the bread in half lengthways and rub all over the cut surfaces with the cut clove of garlic. Brush or sprinkle over the olive oil. Skin and slice the tomatoes and slice the green pepper, discarding the core and seeds. Lay the slices of tomato and pepper on the bread and top with the drained anchovy fillets, capers and olives.
Serves 2-3

Chou vert en paupiettes
Cabbage rolls

8 tender green cabbage leaves
salt
1 1¾-oz can anchovies in olive oil
½ cup cooked rice
2 hard-boiled eggs, finely chopped
1 tablespoon chopped parsley
1 tablespoon chopped chives
freshly milled black pepper
2 tablespoons olive oil
¼ cup black olives

Cook the cabbage leaves in boiling, salted water until they are just tender. Drain and rinse quickly in cold water. Finely chop the anchovy fillets and add to the rice with the oil from the can, hard-boiled eggs, parsley and chives. Season to taste with salt and pepper. Lay the cooked cabbage leaves out flat and trim any very thick pieces at the stem end. Divide the rice mixture into eight portions and place in the center of the cabbage leaves. Turn in the sides of the leaves and roll up so that the filling is completely encased. Arrange the cabbage rolls on a serving dish, sprinkle with the olive oil and more black pepper and garnish with the olives.
Serves 4

Tomates accordéon
Tomato and egg salad

8 medium-sized tomatoes
4 hard-boiled eggs
4 green olives
4 black olives
4 tablespoons *sauce vinaigrette* (see page 52)

Cut the tomatoes into about 6 slices, without cutting through to the base. Shell the eggs and cut each egg into 10 slices, if you have

made 6 cuts in the tomatoes. Put a slice of egg into each cut in the tomato and place the completed tomatoes in a shallow serving dish. Spoon the *sauce vinaigrette* over the tomatoes, then sprinkle with the finely chopped olives.
Serves 4

Champignons à la grecque
Mushrooms stewed in olive oil

⅔ cup water
juice ½ lemon
2 tablespoons olive oil
1 sprig thyme
a bay leaf
1-2 cloves garlic, crushed
1 tablespoon tomato paste
salt and pepper
¾ lb button mushrooms

Put the water, lemon juice, oil, thyme, bay leaf, garlic, tomato paste and seasoning into a sauce pan and bring to the boil. Wash the mushrooms, but do not peel them. Slice them if they are large, but leave whole if small. Add the mushrooms to the pan, cover and simmer gently for about 5 minutes. Remove from the heat, remove thyme and bay leaf, allow to cool and then chill.
Serves 4

Courgettes à la grecque
Zucchini stewed in oil with tomatoes

1 lb zucchini
4 tablespoons olive oil
juice ½ lemon
¾ cup water
1 bay leaf
1 sprig thyme

4 coriander seeds, crushed
1 clove garlic, crushed
salt and pepper
4 large tomatoes, skinned and chopped

Wash the zucchini and cut into diagonal slices about ¾ in thick.
Put the oil, lemon juice, water, bay leaf, thyme, coriander seeds,
garlic, salt and pepper into a saucepan, and bring to the boil. Add
the tomatoes and the zucchini and cook, uncovered, over a
moderate heat for about 25 minutes. Allow the zucchini to cool,
remove the thyme and bay leaf, then chill in the refrigerator for
at least 1 hour before serving.
Serves 4

Ratatouille

2 eggplants
salt
2 onions, finely chopped
4 tablespoons olive oil
2 red or green peppers
4 large tomatoes
2 cloves garlic, crushed
12 coriander seeds, crushed
freshly milled black pepper

Chop the unpeeled eggplants into ½-in cubes, put into a
colander, sprinkle with salt and leave for about 20 minutes for
the excess water to drain off. Put the onions into a pan with the
oil and cook gently for about 10 minutes, or until soft but not
browned. Chop the peppers, discarding the cores and seeds and
add to the pan with the eggplant. Cover and simmer gently for
about 20 minutes. Skin and chop the tomatoes and add to the pan
with the garlic, coriander and pepper and continue cooking for a
further 15 minutes. Remove from the heat, taste and adjust the
seasoning. Serve hot, or allow to cool and then chill.
Serves 4-6

Salade niçoise

There are many, many different recipes for *salade niçoise*, but this is a good basic recipe which you can adapt to what you have in your store-cupboard or larder.

1 large head of lettuce
½ lb cooked green beans
3 tomatoes, quartered
⅓ cup black olives
1 7½-oz can tuna
2 hard-boiled eggs, shelled and quartered
4 tablespoons *sauce vinaigrette* (see page 52)
1 clove garlic, crushed
salt and pepper
1 1¾-oz can anchovy fillets in olive oil

Wash the lettuce, dry and use to line a large salad bowl. Put the beans, tomatoes and most of the olives into a bowl with the drained and flaked tuna, eggs, *sauce vinaigrette* and garlic. Mix well, season with salt and pepper and spoon into the salad bowl. Garnish the top of the dish with the reserved olives and the drained anchovy fillets.
Serves 4

Salade de piments
Red pepper salad

1 medium-sized onion, finely chopped
1 clove garlic, crushed
3 tablespoons olive oil
4 red peppers
salt and pepper

Gently fry the onion and garlic in the oil for about 5 minutes. Cut the peppers into rings, discarding the cores and seeds. Add them to the pan with the seasoning. Cover and simmer gently for 25

minutes. Allow the peppers to cool, then chill for at least 2 hours before serving.
Serves 4

Salade de lentilles
Lentil salad

1 cup lentils (see page 21)
1 *bouquet garni*
salt and pepper
4 tablespoons *sauce vinaigrette* (see page 52)
1 onion, finely chopped
1 tablespoon chopped parsley

Put the lentils into a saucepan with the *bouquet garni* and seasoning and cover with cold water. Bring to the boil, cover and simmer gently for about 1 hour or until the lentils are just tender, but not mushy. Drain and while still hot, add the *sauce vinaigrette*, onion and parsley and mix well. Leave until cold.
Serves 4

Salade de haricots blancs
Haricot bean and tuna salad

1⅓ cups haricot (dried white) beans
2½ cups stock
1 sprig tarragon
1 clove garlic
4 tablespoons *sauce vinaigrette* (see page 52)
1 7½-oz can tuna
1 tablespoon chopped parsley
½ small onion, very finely chopped
salt and pepper

Soak the haricot beans in cold water overnight. Drain. Put into a saucepan with the stock, tarragon and garlic. Cover, bring to the

boil and simmer gently for about 2 hours or until the beans are tender. Drain, and remove the tarragon sprig and garlic. Toss the beans, while they are still warm, in the *sauce vinaigrette* and the oil from the can of tuna, and add the parsley and onion. Season well with salt and pepper and leave to cool. Flake the tuna and mix with the cold beans, then turn into a serving dish.
Serves 4

Salade de haricots verts et d'oeufs
Green bean and egg salad

½ lb green beans
salt
1 clove garlic, crushed
4 tablespoons *sauce vinaigrette* (see page 52)
2 hard-boiled eggs
3 tomatoes
pepper
1 tablespoon chopped chives

Cook the beans in boiling salted water for about 10 minutes. Drain well. Mix the garlic with the *sauce vinaigrette* and toss the beans in this while they are still warm. Allow to cool. Shell and quarter the eggs and quarter the tomatoes. Add to the salad with extra seasoning and mix well. Turn the salad into a serving dish or bowl and sprinkle with chives before serving.
Serves 4

Salade de riz
Mixed rice salad

1 ⅓ cups long-grain rice
salt
1 7½-oz can tuna
1 1¾-oz can anchovies in olive oil
2 tablespoons vinegar

1 teaspoon French mustard
freshly milled black pepper
1 clove garlic, crushed
2 tablespoons chopped chives
2 hard-boiled eggs
4 tomatoes, quartered
⅓ cup black olives
1 tablespoon chopped parsley

Cook the rice in boiling salted water until tender. Drain, rinse in cold water, then mix with the drained oil from the tuna and anchovies, the vinegar, mustard, pepper, garlic and chives, and toss well. Leave to cool. Shell the eggs and cut into quarters and add these to the salad with the flaked tuna, anchovy fillets, tomatoes and olives. Toss lightly, turn into a salad bowl and sprinkle with parsley.
Serves 4

Macédoine provençale
Potato and tomato salad

1 tablespoon capers
1 1¾-oz can anchovies in olive oil
1 tablespoon lemon juice
freshly milled black pepper
1 medium-sized onion, very finely chopped
1 clove garlic, crushed
1 tablespoon finely chopped fennel leaves
½ lb small tomatoes
1 lb cooked new potatoes, sliced
⅓ cup black olives

Pound the capers with the anchovies in a mortar until they form a rough paste, then gradually stir in the lemon juice. Turn into a bowl, add the pepper, onion, garlic and fennel, and mix well.

Add the tomatoes and potatoes to the bowl and toss lightly. Turn into a serving dish and top with the olives.
Serves 4

Salade cévenole
Potato, celery and endive salad

1½ lb potatoes
salt
1 small head celery

½ cup shelled walnuts
¾ cup mayonnaise (see page 50)
pepper
1 small curly endive
2 tablespoons chopped chives

Cook the potatoes in boiling salted water until they are just tender. Drain and, when cool enough to handle, peel, cut into ½-in dice and place in a mixing bowl. Slice the celery and roughly chop the walnuts. Add them to the potatoes with the mayonnaise and seasoning and mix lightly. Leave until the potatoes are quite cold. Before serving, arrange the endive round the outside of a salad bowl, spoon the potato salad into the centre and sprinkle with the chives.
Serves 4

Salade de tomates
Tomato salad

1 clove garlic
1 lb tomatoes, skinned
1 teaspoon chopped basil
½ small onion, very finely chopped
3 tablespoons *sauce vinaigrette* (see page 52)

Cut the garlic clove in half and rub all over the inside of the salad

bowl. Slice the tomatoes thinly and place in the salad bowl. Mix the basil and onion with the *sauce vinaigrette* and pour over the tomatoes. Toss lightly just before serving.
Serves 4

Salade d'oeufs et de pommes de terre
Egg and potato salad

1 lb potatoes
salt
4 hard-boiled eggs
2 teaspoons chopped chives
2 teaspoons chopped parsley
freshly milled black pepper
½ teaspoon French mustard
½ cup + 2 tablespoons *sauce vinaigrette* (see page 52)

Scrub the potatoes, but do not peel them. Cook in boiling salted water until just tender, drain, peel and leave to cool. When cold, cut the potatoes into ½-in dice. Cut the eggs in half and take out the yolks. Pound the yolks with the herbs, seasoning and mustard and gradually beat in the *sauce vinaigrette* a teaspoon at a time. Chop the egg whites coarsely and add them to the potatoes with the sauce. Toss lightly and chill for at least 1 hour before serving.
Serves 4

Salade de flageolets
Flageolet bean salad

1⅓ cups dried *flageolet* or small lima beans
salt
1 *bouquet garni*
¾ cup thin mayonnaise (see page 50)
1 tablespoon chopped parsley
1 onion, finely chopped

Soak the beans in cold water overnight. Drain, put into a sauce-pan with the salt and *bouquet garni* and cover with fresh cold water. Bring to the boil, cover and simmer gently for about 1½ hours or until the beans are just tender. Drain, and while still warm, stir in the mayonnaise, parsley and onion. Leave to cool.
Serves 4

Poireaux vinaigrette
Leeks in French dressing

4 leeks
salt
3 tablespoons *sauce vinaigrette* (see page 52)
2 tablespoons chopped parsley

Remove the outside of the leeks and trim them so that just the white part is left. Wash well in cold water. If the leeks are very large, it may be better to cut them in half lengthways. Cook the leeks in boiling, salted water for about 20 minutes or until they are just tender. Drain well, and leave in the colander for about 5 minutes for the water inside to drain out. Arrange the leeks in a serving dish, then pour over the *sauce vinaigrette* and sprinkle with parsley. Leave for about 2 hours before serving.
Serves 4

Concombres en salade
Cucumber salad

1 cucumber
2 teaspoons salt
2 tablespoons oil
1 teaspoon vinegar
pinch sugar
1 tablespoon chopped chives
1 tablespoon chopped parsley
2 teaspoons chopped dill (if available)

Peel the cucumber with a potato peeler, then slice very thinly. Put the cucumber into a colander, sprinkle with the salt and press it down with a plate. Leave to drain for about 30 minutes, then dry the cucumber well with a clean cloth or paper towel. Put the cucumber into a salad bowl, add the remaining ingredients and toss lightly.
Serves 4

Céleri rémoulade
Celery in rémoulade sauce

1 small head celery
salt
⅔ cup *sauce rémoulade* (see page 51)

Take off the outside stalks of the celery and put these on one side to use for soups and flavouring. Wash the remainder of the celery well and cut diagonally into thin slices. Plunge the celery into boiling salted water for 1 minute, then drain and rinse in cold water. Dry well and blend with the *sauce rémoulade*. Turn into a bowl and serve.
Serves 4

Salade aux artichauts bretonne
Rice and artichoke salad

1 cup rice
salt
4 tablespoons *sauce vinaigrette* (see page 52)
1 clove garlic, crushed
1 14-oz can artichoke hearts or 1 pkge frozen artichoke hearts
    cooked and cooled
2 tablespoons chopped chives

Cook the rice in boiling salted water until just tender. Drain and while still hot toss in the *sauce vinaigrette* and garlic. Leave to

cool. Drain the artichoke hearts and cut in half, add them to the rice and mix lightly. Turn the salad into a serving dish and sprinkle with chives.
Serves 4

Eggs, cheese dishes and savoury flans

Many of the recipes in this chapter make very good, inexpensive lunch or supper dishes. Over the last couple of years there has been an enormous increase in the popularity of savoury flans, such as *quiche Lorraine* and *pissaladière*, and as well as giving recipes for these I have also found a couple of slightly more unusual flans. The *quiche Lorraine* recipe in this chapter can in fact be used as a basis for all sorts of savoury flans: the cheese and bacon can be omitted and replaced by prawns, ham, salmon and chopped green onions, garlic sausages, or anchovies.

Oeufs farcis à la sauce Mornay
Stuffed hard-boiled eggs with cheese sauce

6 hard-boiled eggs
4 tablespoons light cream
1 1¾-oz can anchovies in olive oil
freshly milled black pepper
1 ¼ cups *sauce Mornay* (see page 46)
4 tablespoons grated Gruyère cheese

Cut the hard-boiled eggs in half lengthways. Take out the yolks and mash them with the cream. Drain the anchovies and chop very finely Add them to the egg yolks, mix well and season. Spoon the yolk mixture back into the cases and place the eggs, cut side downwards, in a lightly greased ovenproof serving dish. Pour over the *sauce Mornay* and sprinkle with the cheese.

Bake in a moderately hot oven (400°F) for about 15 minutes or until the cheese is golden brown.
Serves 4

Oeufs farcis provençale
Stuffed hard-boiled'eggs

6 hard-boiled eggs
3 anchovy fillets
1 teaspoon finely chopped capers
1 tablespoon chopped parsley
1¼ cups *sauce bechamel* (see page 45)
pepper and salt
4 tablespoons fresh white breadcrumbs
2 tablespoons butter

Cut the hard-boiled eggs in half lengthways. Take out the yolks and pound them with the anchovies, capers and parsley. Stir in 4 tablespoons of the *sauce bechamel* and season with pepper and salt, if necessary. Pile this mixture back into the egg whites. Pour the rest of the sauce into the bottom of an ovenproof dish and place the eggs on top. Sprinkle with the breadcrumbs and dot with the butter. Bake the eggs in a moderately hot oven (400°F) for 15-20 minutes.
Serves 4

Oeufs à l'ail
Hard-boiled eggs with garlic sauce

10 cloves garlic
2 anchovy fillets
1 teaspoon capers
4 tablespoons olive oil
1 teaspoon vinegar
salt and pepper
6 hard-boiled eggs
2 tablespoons chopped parsley

Peel the garlic, put into a saucepan of boiling water and cook for 10 minutes. Drain and dry the garlic well, then pound in a mortar with the anchovies and capers. Very gradually beat in the oil a drop at a time, then finally the vinegar. Season with pepper, and salt if necessary. Put this sauce in the bottom of a shallow serving dish. Peel the eggs, but leave them whole and arrange on the top of the sauce. Sprinkle with parsley before serving.
Serves 4-6

Oeufs durs au jambon
Hard-boiled eggs with ham

This recipe comes from the Morvan province where Chablis wines are produced. It should be made with Morvan ham which is a local specialty, but ham or bacon can be used.

¾-1 lb lean raw ham or bacon
a calf's foot, preferably; or 2 pig's feet, split in half
1 large onion, chopped
few parsley stalks
6 hard-boiled eggs

Soak the ham or bacon for 2-3 hours in cold water. Put the calf's foot or pig's feet into a saucepan of cold water, bring to the boil and cook for 5 minutes. Drain. Drain the ham and put into a saucepan with 3¾ cups of cold, water, the onion, parsley stalks and calf's foot or pig's feet. Bring slowly to the boil, cover and simmer gently for 1½ hours. Remove from the heat. Shell the eggs, prick them lightly with a fork and put into the saucepan with the ham. Allow to cool. Remove the eggs from the pan and put into a lightly oiled dish or loaf pan. Chop the ham into small pieces and discard any skin and bone. Chop any meat from the calf's foot or pig's feet. Put all the meat into the dish or pan with the eggs. Carefully remove all the grease from the top of the ham liquor, then strain over the eggs. Put into the refrigerator and leave for about 3 hours until the liquor has set into a jelly. To serve, turn out the dish and cut into slices.
Serves 8

Oeufs mollets fines herbes
Soft-boiled eggs with herbs

4 eggs at room temperature
4 tablespoons butter
1 tablespoon chopped parsley
1 tablespoon chopped chives
2 teaspoons lemon juice

Put the eggs into boiling water and cook for exactly 5 minutes. Remove the pan from the heat and place under running cold water. As soon as the eggs are cool enough to handle, lightly tap the shells all over with the back of a spoon. Replace the eggs in the pan and leave under cold running water for a further 2-3 minutes until they are quite cold, then very carefully remove the shells.

Melt the butter in a large shallow pan, add the herbs, eggs and lemon juice and cook, stirring all the time, for about 5 minutes.
Serves 4 as an hors d'oeuvre or 2 as a main course for a light meal

Variation: If preferred, the butter can be replaced with ½ cup + 2 tablespoons of cream. Put this into the pan with the herbs, add the eggs, and heat gently without boiling. Omit the lemon juice.

Oeufs Bénédictine
Eggs Bénédictine

There are several different versions of this recipe: the pastry base can be replaced with slices of toast and the slices of ham with *brandade de morue* (see page 111).

pâte brisée made with 1 cup flour (see page 223)
sauce hollandaise (see page 53)
4 eggs
4 slices ham

Roll the pastry out thinly and use it to line 4 individual tartlet tins, about 4 in in diameter. Cover with parchment paper filled with dried beans and bake in a 400°F oven for 8 minutes. Remove the paper and beans and dry the pastry out in the oven another 5 minutes, then keep warm until required. Pastry cases made in advance can be reheated.

Make the *sauce hollandaise* and keep this warm in the bowl over a pan of hot, *not boiling*, water. Poach the eggs and very lightly grill the ham. To assemble the dish, lay a slice of ham in the bottom of each tartlet case, put a poached egg on top and spoon over the *sauce hollandaise*. Serve as soon as possible.
Serves 4 as an hors d'oeuvre or 2 as a main course

Oeufs durs à la brettone
Hard-boiled eggs with haricot beans

Follow the recipe for cooking the beans on page 191, but add 8 shelled hard-boiled eggs to the tomato mixture with the beans.

Oeufs en cocotte à la crème
Baked eggs with cream

Eggs cooked in this way can be simply superb, or — if not well cooked — quite revolting, so it is worth while taking a few pains to make sure you have followed the recipe carefully.

butter
4 tablespoons light or heavy cream
4 eggs
salt and pepper

Lightly butter 4 individual ramekin or cocotte dishes and pour a tablespoonful of cream into the bottom of each. Stand the dishes in a roasting pan containing 1 in of hot water, put into a moderate oven (350°F) and leave for about 10 minutes. Remove from the oven and carefully break an egg into each dish, season with salt and pepper. Cover the dishes with foil and bake for

about 10 minutes or until the whites are just set, but the yolks still soft.
Serves 4 as an hors d'oeuvre or 2 as a main course

Oeufs en cocotte au pâté
Baked eggs with pâté

Put a tablespoonful of pâté into the bottom of each dish, pour over the cream and continue as above.

Oeufs en cocotte aux crevettes
Baked eggs with prawns

Put a tablespoonful of cooked prawns or shrimps in the bottom of each dish, pour over the cream and continue as above.

Pipérade
Scrambled eggs with peppers and tomatoes

This is a famous recipe from the Basque region of France. It is one of those dishes which does not look very appetizing, but tastes delicious.

4 red peppers
1 lb tomatoes
6 tablespoons butter
1 onion, finely chopped
2 cloves garlic, crushed
8 eggs
salt and pepper

Cut the peppers into ½-in pieces, discarding the cores and seeds. Skin the tomatoes, then cut them into quarters and remove the seeds. Melt the butter in a pan and fry the onion, garlic and peppers gently for about 5 minutes. Add the tomatoes and con-

tinue cooking for a further 10 minutes. Meanwhile beat the eggs in a basin and season with salt and pepper. Pour the egg mixture into the saucepan and cook gently over a low heat until the eggs are scrambled. Serve hot or cold.
Serves 4

Omelettes

These days very few of us keep a special omelette pan in the cupboard and never use it for anything else. With the advent of non-stick pans, the long and tedious process of 'seasoning' a pan before cooking omelettes in it is no longer necessary. If, however, you do not have a non-stick pan and need to season a pan before cooking, this is what you do: first rub the inside of the pan all over with salt so that it is really clean, then wipe out with a paper towel. Put a knob of lard into the pan and put over a moderate heat until it begins to smoke. Remove the pan from the heat, pour off the lard and wipe the pan out with paper.

The only other important point about the pan for an omelette is the size; for a 2-egg omelette you should use a 6 to 7-in diameter pan, or the omelette will be too thin and dry.

2 eggs
2 teaspoons water
salt and freshly milled black pepper
1 tablespoon butter

Lightly beat the eggs, water and seasoning with a fork until they are blended. Put the butter into the pan and heat until it is foaming. Pour in all the egg mixture at once. Tip the pan and stir the egg lightly with a fork pushing the cooked part into the centre. When the underside is golden brown, and the top still moist and creamy, loosen the edges with a spatula and tip the pan away from you with a jerk so that the omelette folds over itself. Slide the omelette onto a heated plate and serve immediately.
Serves 1

Omelette aux fines herbes
Herb omelette

Add 2 teaspoons chopped parsley, 1 teaspoon chopped chives and a pinch chopped tarragon, if liked, to the eggs before cooking.

Omelette au fromage
Cheese omelette

Add 6 tablespoons grated Gruyère cheese to the omelette just before folding.

Omelette au jambon et aux fines herbes
Ham omelette with herbs

Add 2 teaspoons chopped parsley and 1 teaspoon chopped chives to the eggs before cooking. Add ⅓ cup lean ham to the omelette just before folding.

Omelette aux champignons
Mushroom omelette

Finely chop 5 or 6 mushrooms and fry in 2 tablespoons butter. Stir in 2 teaspoons chopped parsley and add to the omelette just before folding.

Omelette Parmentier
Potato omelette

Thinly slice a small cooked potato and fry in 2 tablespoons butter until crisp and golden. Sprinkle with a pinch of chopped rosemary and add to the omelette just before folding.

Omelette aux anchois et au fromage
Anchovy and cheese omelette

Very finely chop 2 anchovy fillets and add these to the eggs before cooking with 2 teaspoons chopped parsley. Add 4 tablespoons grated Gruyère cheese just before folding.

Omelette provençale
Ratatouille omelette

Add 2 tablespoons cooked *ratatouille* (see page 62) to the omelette just before folding.

Soufflés

A great deal of unnecessary mystique is attached to the making of soufflés. If you analyse what you do when making the savoury soufflés given here, you only have to make a straightforward sauce, add the flavouring you require and the egg yolks, and then fold in the stiffly beaten egg whites. The only point that requires some care is the egg whites which must be so stiffly beaten that you really can turn the bowl upside down without them shifting. But watch that they are not too stiffly beaten and consequently dry as this makes them very difficult to fold into the sauce mixture, with the result that you end up stirring them in and a great deal of air is lost. As a cheese soufflé is the one most commonly made I have used this as the basic recipe.

Soufflé au fromage
Cheese soufflé

2 tablespoons butter
4 tablespoons flour
¾ cup milk

¾ cup grated Gruyère cheese
4 tablespoons grated Parmesan cheese
4 eggs, separated
salt and freshly milled black pepper
½ teaspoon strong French mustard

Melt the butter in a large saucepan, add the flour and cook for about 1 minute. Gradually blend in the milk and bring to the boil, stirring all the time until the sauce is thick and smooth. Remove from the heat and stir in the cheese. Beat the egg yolks in one at a time and season with salt, pepper and mustard. Beat the egg whites stiffly until they form soft peaks, then carefully fold into the sauce mixture. Turn into a buttered 1½ quart soufflé dish and bake in a moderately hot oven (375°F) for about 30 minutes or until well risen and golden brown.
Serves 2-4 for a main course or 4-5 as a starter

Soufflé au fromage et aux épinards
Cheese and spinach soufflé

Make as the cheese soufflé, above, but omit the Parmesan cheese and reduce the Gruyère cheese to 4 tablespoons. Add ⅔ cup finely chopped, cooked spinach and a pinch grated nutmeg with the egg yolks.

Soufflé au fromage et aux poireaux
Cheese and leek soufflé

Cut 1 lb leeks into 1-in pieces and cook in boiling salted water until just tender. Drain, then put into a saucepan with 1 table-spoon of butter and put over a gentle heat until they are quite dry. Make the soufflé as the cheese soufflé, above, but omit the Parmesan cheese and reduce the Gruyère cheese to 4 tablespoons. Add the leeks with the egg yolks.

Soufflé au fromage et au jambon
Cheese and ham soufflé

Finely chop a shallot and fry in 1 tablespoon butter until transparent. Add ¾ cup finely chopped ham and 1 tablespoon chopped parsley. Make the soufflé as the cheese soufflé, above, but add the ham mixture with the egg yolks. Omit the Parmesan cheese and reduce the Gruyère cheese to 4 tablespoons.

Soufflé aux champignons
Mushroom soufflé

Finely chop ¼ lb of mushrooms and 1 shallot. Cook gently in 2 tablespoons of butter for about 10 minutes, then add 1 tablespoon chopped parsley. Make the soufflé as the cheese soufflé above, but add the mushroom mixture with the egg yolks. Omit the cheese and mustard.

Soufflé au crabe
Crab soufflé

Put 1¼ cups of milk into a saucepan with a tiny piece of bay leaf, a piece of carrot, ½ chopped onion, ⅛ teaspoon mace and a few parsley stalks. Bring slowly to the boil, cover and simmer gently for 10 minutes, then strain. Make the soufflé as the cheese soufflé, above, but use this milk in place of that given in the recipe and add 6 oz fresh crab meat, or use a 7½-oz can crab meat, well drained, and a good pinch of cayenne pepper with the egg yolks. Omit the cheese.

Gougère
Cheese choux pastry

This light cheese dish comes from Burgundy and can either be served warm on its own as an *hors d'oeuvre* or a savoury, or be filled as in the recipes below. *Gougère* is also excellent made into very small puffs and served with drinks.

½ cup + 2 tablespoons flour
¼ teaspoon salt
freshly milled black pepper
4 tablespoons butter
⅔ cup water
¾ cup finely grated Gruyère cheese
3 eggs

Sift the flour, salt and pepper together. Put the butter, cut into small pieces, into a pan with the water. Bring slowly to the boil. Remove the pan from the heat, add the flour all at once and beat well until the mixture forms a soft ball that leaves the sides of the pan clean. If necessary, return the pan to a very gentle heat for about a minute. Allow to cool for a few minutes; beat in the cheese, then the eggs, one at a time. Put tablespoonfuls of the mixture, fairly wide apart, on greased baking sheets and bake in a hot oven (425°F) for about 20 minutes or until golden brown. Remove from the oven and serve warm.
Serves 4

Gougère aux poireaux
Cheese choux pastry with leeks

gougère mixture (see above)
1½ lb leeks
salt
2 tablespoons butter
4 tablespoons flour
1¼ cups milk

Make the *gougère* as above, but spread half of it in the bottom of a greased ovenproof dish. Pile the rest in spoonfuls round the edge and bake in a hot oven (425°F) for 20 minutes. Cover the top lightly with foil and continue baking for about another 10

minutes. While the *gougère* is cooking, clean the leeks and cut into pieces about 1 in long. Cook in boiling salted water until just tender. Drain and reserve the liquid. Melt the butter in a pan, add the flour and cook for a minute. Stir in the milk and bring to the boil, stirring all the time. Add ⅔ cup of the liquid from cooking the leeks, and the leeks themselves. Heat gently, then taste and adjust the seasoning. Spoon this sauce into the centre of the baked *gougère* just before serving.
Serves 4

Gougère aux épinards
Cheese choux pastry with spinach

gougère mixture (see page 84)
4 tablespoons butter
2 lb fresh spinach
salt
1 small onion, finely chopped
1 small green pepper, finely chopped
½ cup + 2 tablespoons heavy cream
pinch grated nutmeg

Make the *gougère* as above, but spread half of it into the bottom of a greased ovenproof dish. Pile the rest in spoonfuls round the edge and bake in a hot oven (425°F) for 20 minutes. Cover the top lightly with foil and continue baking for about another 10 minutes. While the *gougère* is cooking, melt 2 tablespoons of the butter in a large saucepan, add the well-washed spinach and a good pinch of salt, cover and cook for about 15 minutes or until the spinach is tender. Drain the spinach well and chop finely. Melt the remaining butter in a pan and gently fry the onion and pepper for about 10 minutes. Add the spinach, cream, nutmeg and seasoning and heat gently, without boiling. Spoon this mixture into the centre of the baked *gougère* just before serving.
Serves 4

Pannequets au jambon
Savoury stuffed pancakes with ham

1 ¼ cups unsweetened pancake batter (see page 212)
4 tablespoons butter
1 large onion, finely chopped
½ lb mushrooms, finely chopped
¾ cup finely chopped cooked ham
salt and pepper

Using the batter make 8 pancakes, following the instructions on page 213. Melt half the butter in a saucepan and gently fry the onion for about 5 minutes. Add the mushrooms and the ham, and cook, uncovered, for about 10 minutes. Season well with salt and pepper. Put a good tablespoon of the ham mixture in the centre of each pancake, roll up and place in an ovenproof dish. Melt the remaining butter and spoon over the pancakes. Heat through in a moderate oven (350°F) for about 25 minutes.
Serves 4

Croque monsieur
Cheese and ham sandwich

This makes a very good lunchtime snack.

2 slices white bread
butter
1 slice cooked ham
½ teaspoon French mustard (optional)
1 slice Gruyère cheese

Remove the crusts from the bread, and butter one side of each slice. Lay the slice of ham on the buttered side of one piece of bread and spread with the mustard, if wished. Lay the cheese and the second slice of bread on top. Either fry the sandwich in butter on both sides until golden, or put under a hot grill until golden brown on both sides.
Makes 1 sandwich

Canapés au fromage
Toasted cheese

This is rather like a cross between Welsh rarebit and cheesy scrambled egg.

2 slices white bread
1 egg
4 oz soft cream cheese
½ cup grated Gruyère cheese
salt and pepper

Cut the crusts off the bread and toast lightly on both sides. Lightly beat the egg, then blend in the cream cheese, Gruyère cheese and seasoning. Turn into a saucepan and cook over a gentle heat until thick. Spread the mixture over the toast, leaving about ¼ in all the way round the edge. Broil under a moderate flame until golden brown.
Serves 2

Poireaux au jambon, sauce Mornay
Leeks with ham and cheese sauce

8 medium-sized leeks
salt
1¼ cups *sauce Mornay* (see method)
8 thin slices ham
4 tablespoons grated Gruyère cheese
2 tablespoons fresh white breadcrumbs

Remove the outside leaves, roots and most of the green part of the leeks. Wash well in cold water to remove all the grit and dirt. Cook the leeks in boiling salted water until tender, drain and reserve ⅔ cup of the cooking liquid. Make the *sauce Mornay* (as page 46), but use ⅔ cup of the reserved cooking liquid in place of ⅔ cup of the milk.

Wrap a slice of ham round each leek. Top with the sauce and

sprinkle with the cheese and breadcrumbs. Place under a moderate flame and broil until golden brown and bubbling.
Serves 4

Fondue savoyarde
Cheese fondue

Cheese *fondue* is not just a Swiss specialty but is made in the French Alps as well.

1 clove garlic, peeled
2½ cups dry white wine
1 lb Emmenthal cheese, grated
1 tablespoon cornstarch or, preferably, potato flour
2 tablespoons Kirsch
1 large French loaf

Peel the garlic clove and cut it in half, then rub the garlic all over the inside of the pan. Put all but about 3 tablespoons of the wine into the pan and bring to the boil; lower the heat and gradually stir in the cheese. Blend the remaining wine with the cornstarch or potato flour, and quickly stir this into the mixture, then add the Kirsch. Cook for about 5 minutes.

Keep the *fondue* warm, either over a spirit stove or over a very low heat on the stove. Cut the bread into cubes, about 1 in square and serve with the *fondue*.
Serves 6

Quiche Lorraine

As with so many other dishes which have become popular, recipes for *quiche Lorraine* vary enormously and most Lorrainers would probably be horrified to see what passes as *quiche Lorraine* in many foreign shops and restaurants. The original basic recipe consisted only of bacon, eggs and cream, without the Gruyère cheese, which is now generally considered a basic ingredient, and which I personally think makes it much nicer.

pâte brisée made with 1 cup flour (see page 223)
4 oz Gruyère cheese, thinly sliced (optional) — 3 pieces
6 strips lean bacon, halved
2 eggs
½ cup + 2 tablespoons light cream
salt and pepper   dash nutmeg

Roll out the pastry and use to line a 9-in shallow flan ring or pan.
Lay the slices of cheese in the bottom of the flan case and top with
the bacon. Beat the eggs, then beat in the cream and seasoning.
Pour into the flan case. Bake in a moderate oven (350°F) for
about 30 minutes. Serve hot or cold.
Serves 4-6

Tarte à l'oignon
Onion tart

French or Spanish onions give this dish a much richer flavour.

pâte brisée made with 1 cup flour (see page 223)
1 ½ lb onions, preferably large ones
4 tablespoons butter
3 eggs
½ cup + 2 tablespoons heavy cream
salt and freshly milled black pepper
good pinch grated nutmeg

Roll out the pastry and use to line a 9-in flan ring or pan. Peel the
onions and slice very thinly. Melt the butter in a pan, add the
onions and cook gently, uncovered, until soft and golden. This
will take about 30 minutes as if it is not done gently the onions
will burn; they should be stirred several times during cooking.
Beat the eggs with the cream, plenty of seasoning and nutmeg;
then add the onions and mix well. Spoon carefully into the prepared pastry case and bake in a moderate oven (350°F) for about
30 minutes.
Serves 4-6

Tarte aux épinards
Spinach tart

pâte brisée made with 1 cup flour (see page 223)
2 tablespoons butter
1 medium-sized onion, finely chopped
2 eggs
⅔ cup light cream
1½ cups cooked spinach, finely chopped, or use a 10-oz package of frozen spinach, thawed and well drained
salt and pepper
½ teaspoon grated nutmeg
6 oz Gruyère cheese, thinly sliced

Roll out the pastry and use to line a 9-in flan ring or pan. Melt the butter in a small pan and fry the onion gently for about 5 minutes. Beat the eggs with the cream, then stir in the onion and spinach. Season with salt, pepper and nutmeg. Lay half the slices of cheese in the bottom of the flan. Spoon the spinach mixture over them and top with the remaining sliced cheese. Bake in a moderate oven (350°F) for 30 minutes or until golden brown.
Serves 4-6

Pissaladière
Tomato and onion flan

This is a recipe from Provence and is very similar to the Italian pizzas; a yeast dough is very often used instead of the *pâte brisée* given here.

pâte brisée made with 1 cup flour (see page 223)
4 tablespoons olive oil
2 large onions, chopped
1 lb tomatoes, skinned and chopped
1 tablespoon tomato paste
2 cloves garlic, crushed

1 sprig rosemary
salt and freshly milled black pepper
2 tablespoons grated Parmesan cheese
1 1 ¾-oz can anchovies in olive oil
black olives

Roll out the pastry and use to line a 9-in flan ring or pan. Fill the flan with buttered foil and baking beans and bake in a moderately hot oven (400°F) for 10-15 minutes until the pastry is set. Remove the foil and beans and bake for a further 5 minutes to dry out the base.

Heat the oil in a saucepan and fry the onions over a gentle heat for about 10 minutes. Add the tomatoes, tomato paste, garlic, rosemary and seasoning. Cover and simmer for about 20 minutes, then cook in an open pan for about 10 minutes, stirring until thick. Remove the rosemary sprig.

Sprinkle the base of the flan case with the Parmesan cheese and spoon over the tomato mixture. Cut the anchovy fillets in half lengthways and arrange in a lattice over the top of the flan. Brush all over the top of the tomato mixture with the oil from the anchovy can. Arrange olives in the squares of the lattice. Bake in a moderate oven (350°F) for about 20 minutes and serve piping hot.
Serves 4

Tarte aux champignons
Mushroom flan

pâte brisée made with 1 cup flour (see page 223)
1 ¼ cups *sauce béchamel* (see method)
½ lb button mushrooms, quartered
2 tablespoons butter
3 tablespoons heavy cream
¾ cup grated Gruyère or Emmenthal cheese
salt and pepper

Roll out the pastry and use to line a 9-in flan ring or pan. Fill the centre with buttered foil and baking beans and bake in a moderately hot oven (400°F) for 15 minutes. Remove the foil and beans and bake for a further 5 minutes to dry out the base.

Make the *sauce béchamel* (see page 45) but use 1¼ cups of milk to make a rather thicker sauce. Fry the mushrooms gently in the butter for about 10 minutes and season with salt and pepper. Stir the cream and cheese into the *sauce béchamel* together with the drained liquid from cooking the mushrooms. Spoon the mushrooms into the bottom of the flan case and pour the sauce over them. Replace in the oven and cook for a further 15 minutes or until golden brown.
Serves 4-6

Tarte aux tomates
Tomato flan

This flan could not be simpler to make, and is ideal for taking on summer picnics.

pâte brisée made with 1 cup flour (see page 223)
1 lb tomatoes
salt
½ lb Gruyère cheese, grated
½ cup + 2 tablespoons light cream
⅓ cup black olives

Roll out the pastry and use to line a 9-in flan ring or pan. Prick the base lightly with a fork and fill the flan with a sheet of buttered foil and baking beans. Bake in a moderately hot oven (400°F) for 15 minutes. Remove the foil and beans and bake for a further 5 minutes to dry out the base.

While the pastry is cooking, thickly slice the tomatoes, place on a rack with a plate underneath and sprinkle with salt so that the excess liquid drains out. Mix the grated cheese with the cream and spoon this into the baked flan case. Lay the tomato slices on

top and sprinkle fairly generously with black pepper. Place the olives in between the tomato slices. Bake in the oven for 15 minutes or until the tomatoes are cooked. Serve hot or cold.
Serves 4-6

Pâtés, terrines and galantines

There is nothing to equal French *charcuterie* — even the smallest villages can often boast both a *boucher* and a *charcutier* who will sell pâtés, terrines, salamis, smoked sausages, fresh pork sausages, chitterlings, black and white puddings, local smoked ham, headcheese, etc. The type will vary from region to region and unfortunately (or fortunately) you will have to visit France to taste many of them, as — apart from the pates, salamis, hams and various canned products — very little is exported.

All the recipes I have given in this chapter are very simple ones — I have not gone into the realms of *pâté de foie gras truffé* as I felt it was unlikely that many readers would have a sufficiently large quantity of goose livers around to make it! Remember when making pâtés and terrines that if you leave them for a couple of days before eating the flavour will mature and improve. They can be kept for a couple of weeks in a refrigerator if you seal them with melted pork fat or butter immediately after cooking. It is important, though, to make quite sure that the fat does completely encase the pâté as this prevents the air, and consequently the bacteria, from coming in contact with the meat. Pâtés and terrines also freeze well so if you have the time, and enough containers, it is a good idea to make up two while you are cooking, and freeze one of them. Always allow plenty of time for them to defrost in either a refrigerator or a cold place, as this helps to retain the maximum flavour.

Pâté de foie simple
Simple liver pâté

¼ lb chicken livers
¼ lb fat bacon
1 small onion, chopped
1 clove garlic, crushed
½ cup butter
⅔ cup *sauce béchamel* (see page 45)
1 teaspoon strong French mustard
salt and pepper

Gently fry the liver, bacon, onion and garlic in half the butter for about 10 minutes. Remove from the heat and either put into a blender with the sauce for a few minutes, or grind the meat mixture then add to the sauce. Add the mustard and season to taste with salt and pepper. Turn the mixture into a small, well-greased terrine, cover with foil and a lid. Stand the dish in a roasting pan containing 1 in of cold water and bake in a moderate oven (350°F) for 1 hour. Remove from the oven and leave to cool. Melt the remaining butter in a pan, then strain through a fine sieve onto the cold pâté. Store in a cold larder or refrigerator until required.
Serves 4-6

Pâté de foie de volaille
Chicken liver pâté

10 tablespoons butter
1 small onion, very finely chopped
1 clove garlic, crushed
½ lb. chicken livers
1 sprig thyme
1 tablespoon brandy
salt and pepper

Melt 2 tablespoons of the butter in a pan and gently fry the onion

and garlic with the thyme for 5 minutes. Add the liver to the pan and cook quickly for about 5 more minutes, then remove from the heat. Allow the mixture to cool slightly, then either chop roughly and put into a blender and blend until smooth, or grind the mixture, then pass through a sieve. Lightly cream 6 table-spoons of the remaining butter and beat in the liver mixture. Add the brandy, and season to taste. Pack the pâté into a small china pot. Melt the remaining butter in a pan, allow to cool slightly, then strain over the pâté.
Serves 4

Pâté de campagne
Country-style pâté

2 bay leaves
6 strips lean bacon
2 cups fresh white breadcrumbs
2 eggs
⅔ cup red wine
2 cloves garlic, crushed
½ lb fresh pork belly
½ lb fat bacon
1 lb pork liver
1 lb chicken liver
2 teaspoons chopped thyme
1 teaspoon chopped sage
1 tablespoon chopped parsley
1 ½ teaspoons grated nutmeg
salt and pepper

Well-grease a large terrine or loaf pan and arrange the bay leaves on the bottom. Cut any rind off the bacon and stretch the bacon on a board with the back of a knife. Use this bacon to line the bottom and sides of the terrine. Mix together the breadcrumbs, eggs, wine and garlic. Finely grind the pork belly, fat bacon (dis-carding all the rind), and the livers. Add to the bread with the remaining ingredients and mix well. Turn into the prepared terrine or pan and cover with foil and a lid, if using a terrine. Stand in a roasting pan containing 1 in cold water and bake in a very moderate oven (325°F) for 2½ hours. Remove from the oven and place weights on top of the foil to press it down. Allow to cool and then chill. Turn out of the dish when ready to serve. *Serves 10-12*

Pâté Périgord
Pork liver pâté, Périgord style

This is rather an unusual pâté in that a pig's foot and additional vegetables are placed on top of the pâté during cooking, which give extra flavour and also make a delicious meat jelly round the edge of it.

6 strips bacon
1 lb pork liver
1 lb salt pork
4 shallots
3 cloves garlic, crushed
freshly milled black pepper
2 tablespoons brandy
¼ teaspoon grated nutmeg
¼ teaspoon ground cloves
1 pig's foot, split in two
2 medium-sized carrots, sliced
2 medium-sized onions, sliced
1 *bouquet garni*
½ cup white wine
½ cup water

Cut any rind off the bacon strips and stretch them with the back of a knife on a board. Use to line the base and sides of a terrine or other suitable container. Grind the liver with the pork and shallots. Pound with a wooden spoon in a bowl and add the

garlic, pepper, brandy, nutmeg and cloves. Spoon into the prepared terrine. Place the pig's foot, carrots, onions, and *bouquet
garni* on top, pour over the wine and water. Cover tightly with
foil and a lid and stand the terrine in a roasting pan containing 1
in of cold water. Cook in a very moderate oven (325°F) for 4
hours. Take the terrine out of the oven, remove and discard the
pig's foot, carrots, onion and *bouquet garni*. Leave to cool.
Serves 8-10

Terrine de poulet au citron
Chicken terrine with lemon

This is a very simple chicken terrine which is excellent with salad.

1 3-4 lb chicken
¾ lb. fresh pork belly
2 onions
2 cloves garlic, crushed
2 tablespoons chopped parsley
grated zest and juice 1 small lemon
1 egg, beaten
salt and pepper

Remove the breast meat from the chicken, cut into neat strips,
and put on one side. Take the rest of the chicken meat off the
bones and grind it with the chicken liver and heart, the pork and
onions. Put into a bowl and add the remaining ingredients. Mix
well. Put half the ground mixture into a well-greased terrine. Lay
the strips of chicken breast on top and then cover with the remaining chicken and pork mixture. Cover the terrine with foil
and a lid. Stand in a roasting pan containing 1 in of cold water
and cook in a very moderate oven (325°F) for 2½ hours. Remove
from the oven and place weights on top of the chicken to press it
while it cools. Serve, cut in slices.
Serves 8

Terrine de canard
Duck terrine

1 4 lb duck
2 tablespoons brandy
¾ lb stewing veal
¾ lb lean pork
1 large egg
salt and freshly milled black pepper
2 tablespoons chopped parsley
1 teaspoon fresh thyme

Take all the duck off the bones and cut about a quarter of it into neat strips. Put this into a dish with the brandy and leave to marinate for 2 hours. Grind all the remaining duck flesh with about half the duck skin and fat, and the veal and pork. Put into a bowl and mix with the egg, seasoning and herbs. Blend well. Spoon half the ground mixture into the bottom of a greased terrine. Lay the strips of duck on the top, then cover with the remaining ground mixture. Cover the terrine or dish with foil and a lid, if possible. Stand in a roasting pan containing 1 in cold water and bake in a very moderate oven (325°F) for 2 hours. Remove the dish from the oven and put weights on top of the foil as the terrine cools. Put the remainder of the duck fat into a small saucepan and put over low heat until the fat has melted, then spoon this over the cold terrine to seal it. Store in the refrigerator or a cold place.
Serves 4-6

Terrine de lièvre ou de lapin
Hare or rabbit terrine

1 small hare or 1 large rabbit
½ lb lean pork
½ lb fat salt pork
1 large onion

1 tablespoon chopped parsley
1 teaspoon chopped fresh thyme
2 cloves garlic, crushed
salt and freshly milled black pepper
4 tablespoons red wine
2 tablespoons brandy or use 2 extra tablespoons of wine
4 strips lean bacon

Bone the hare or rabbit and cut the meat from the back carefully into strips. This is a rather long and tedious process, but it will be made a great deal easier if you use a small, very sharp knife. Put the meat from the back carefully on one side and grind the remainder with the pork and onion. Add the parsley, thyme, garlic, seasoning, wine, and brandy, if used, and mix well. Place half the mixture in the bottom of a large, well-greased terrine or dish. Lay the reserved strips of meat from the back of the hare and the strips of lean bacon on top, then spoon over the remainder of the ground mixture. Cover the dish with foil and then a lid. Stand the dish in a roasting pan containing 1 in cold water and bake in a slow oven (325°F) for 2½ hours. Remove from the oven, take off the lid and place weights on top of the foil to press the terrine down. Allow to cool, then store in the refrigerator until required.
Serves 8-12
Note: The bones from the hare or rabbit can be used to make stock (see page 27).

Terrine de porc
Pork terrine

8 strips lean bacon
1 lb pork tenderloin
2 tablespoons butter
1 small onion, finely chopped
¼ lb mushrooms, finely chopped
¼ lb pork liver

¼ lb pork belly
⅔ cup fresh white breadcrumbs
1 tablespoon brandy
½ teaspoon finely chopped thyme
1 tablespoon chopped parsley
salt and freshly milled black pepper

Cut off any rind from the bacon strips. Place the strips on a board and stretch them with the back of a knife. Use six of them to line the base and sides of a terrine or loaf pan. Slit the pork tenderloin, place between two sheets of wax paper and beat with a mallet or rolling pin to flatten. Melt the butter in a saucepan and gently fry the onion for 5 minutes. Add the mushrooms and cook for a further 4 minutes. Grind the liver and fat pork together and add to the onion and mushrooms with the remaining ingredients. Mix well. Put a third of the ground mixture in the prepared terrine or pan and cover with half the pork tenderloin, then a layer of ground mixture, the remaining pork tenderloin and finally the last of the ground mixture. Lay the remaining bacon strips on top. Cover tightly with foil and a lid. Stand the terrine in a roasting pan containing 1 in. hot water and bake in a very moderate oven (325°F) for 2½ hours. Take out of the oven and stand a weight on top of the foil to press the terrine while it is cooling.
Serves 8-12

Rillettes de porc
Potted pork

Rillettes can be found in *charcuteries* all over France and vary slightly from region to region, but the most famous of all come from Tours.

4 lb pork belly
1 sprig thyme
2 cloves garlic
salt and pepper

Remove the skin and any bones from the pork and cut into
½-in cubes. Put into an ovenproof dish with the thyme, garlic
and seasoning. Cover and cook in a very slow oven (300°F) for 3
hours. Place a sieve over a bowl and turn the pork mixture into
the sieve. Discard any large pieces of pork fat, then roughly mash
the meat, a little at a time, using two forks to tear it apart. Pack
the pork firmly into 1 large or several smaller pots, then pour all
the strained juices and fat over the top of the *rilletes* to seal them.
This will keep for several weeks in a refrigerator.
Serves 8

Rillettes de lapin
Potted pork and rabbit

1 lb salt pork
2 lb rabbit
few peppercorns
1 sprig thyme
2 cloves garlic
1 small bay leaf

Cut off the skin from the pork, put the pork into a pan of cold
water and leave to soak for about 8 hours, drain. Cut the pork
into 2-in cubes and disjoint the rabbit. Put the pork and rabbit
into an ovenproof dish with the remaining ingredients. Cover
and cook in a very slow oven (300°F) for 4 hours or until the
rabbit comes very easily off the bone. Place a sieve over a bowl
and turn the pork and rabbit mixture into the sieve. Discard any
large pieces of pork fat, and take the pork and rabbit off the
bones. Using two forks on a board, roughly mash the meat a little
at a time and pack firmly into a small terrine. Pour over all the
juices and fat from the bowl to seal it and leave in a cold place.
Serves 6-8

Ballottine de canard à l'orange
Stuffed duck with orange

This recipe sounds very complicated — and boning a duck does take time, especially on your first attempt — but I think you will find the end result worth it. The other advantages are that one duck will serve 8 people comfortably, whereas it would normally only serve about 4, and it is much easier to carve.

1 duck, about 4-5 lb
salt and pepper
¼ teaspoon chopped rosemary
1 teaspoon chopped marjoram
3 oranges
3 tablespoons butter
6 oz lean pork
6 oz stewing veal
2 tablespoons brandy
1 ¼ cups white wine

Put the duck, breast-side down, on a wooden board. With a sharp knife cut through the back skin and flesh to the backbone, then carefully work the flesh away from the carcass, pressing the knife closely against the carcass and taking all the meat away from the bone with the skin. Remove the bones from the legs and wings by scraping the flesh away from the bones, but take great care not to split the skin. Leave the drumstick bones in place. When all the bones have been removed, lay the duck out flat and remove any excess fat, then sprinkle with salt, pepper and the herbs. Peel the oranges so that all the white pith is removed, then cut them in half lengthways. Melt the butter in a small pan and fry the duck liver for about 4 minutes. Remove from the pan and grind it with the pork and veal. Put the ground mixture into a bowl with the brandy, 1 tablespoon of the wine, and salt and pepper. Mix well. Spread half of this onto the duck, then lay the orange halves along the centre of the duck with their cut sides uppermost. Spread the remaining ground mixture on top. Fold in the ends of the duck, then fold the sides into the centre to form a

parcel. Sew together with fine string or coarse thread. Turn the duck breastside up and place in a roasting pan. Sprinkle with salt and pepper and pour over the rest of the wine. Roast in a moderate oven (350°F) for 2 hours. Remove from the oven and allow to cool. This duck looks particularly attractive if you arrange it on a serving dish, cut off about 4 slices and lay these out in front of the duck.
Serves 8

Fromage de tête
Headcheese

Headcheese is quite a performance to make, but a pig's head can be bought very cheaply and the end result will be well worth the effort.

1 pig's head
2 pig's feet
3 onions
3 carrots
3 leeks
2 cloves garlic
1 bay leaf
2 sprigs parsley
2 sprigs thyme
8 white peppercorns
2 tablespoons wine vinegar
1 tablespoon salt
⅔ cup red wine
water

Ask the butcher to chop the head into about five pieces for you. Put into a large pan with the pig's feet, onions, carrots, leeks, garlic, bay leaf, parsley, thyme, peppercorns, vinegar and salt. Pour in enough water to cover the meat and bring slowly to the boil. Remove any scum that comes to the surface, cover the pan with, first, a sheet of foil, then the lid, and simmer very gently for

about 6 hours. It is important that the liquid really does only simmer very gently and, if you prefer, you can put it into a very slow oven (275°F) instead. Drain off the liquid and reserve; discard the vegetables. Remove all the meat from the bones and chop it into ½-in pieces, but keep the tongue whole. Put 3¾ cups of the reserved cooking stock into a clean pan with the red wine and boil rapidly until it is reduced to 2 cups. Taste and adjust the seasoning. Replace the meat in the reduced stock and wine and simmer gently for 30 minutes, then remove from the heat and taste and adjust the seasoning again. Leave the meat and stock until it is cold and almost set, then spoon half the chopped meat into a pan, place the tongue along the middle, then add the rest of the chopped meat. Pour the stock over and leave until set. Turn out of the pan before serving.
Serves 8

Galantine de boeuf et de jambon
Glazed beef and ham galantine

1¼ lb lean chuck beef
½ lb cooked ham
1⅓ cups fresh white breadcrumbs
1 tablespoon chopped parsley
¼ teaspoon chopped thyme
salt and pepper
2 eggs, lightly beaten
To glaze and garnish:
⅔ cup aspic jelly (see page 28)
1 hard-boiled egg, sliced
1 large tomato, sliced

Grind the beef and ham together, then mix with the breadcrumbs, herbs and seasoning. Bind together with the beaten eggs. Turn the mixture into a well-greased loaf pan and cover with a double layer of foil. Stand the tin in a roasting pan containing 1 in of cold water and bake in a very moderate oven (325°F) for 2 hours. Remove the pan from the oven and place weights on top of the foil to press the galantine down while it is cooling. As soon as it is cool, chill in the refrigerator for at least a couple of hours.

Turn the galantine out of the pan onto a wire rack with a plate underneath to catch any drips. Spoon a little of the cold aspic all over the galantine and leave it to set. Pour a little of the aspic jelly into a saucer, dip the slices of egg and tomato into this, then arrange them attractively over the top of the galantine. Leave until they are set, then spoon over the last of the aspic.
Serves 6-8

Galantine de veau
Veal galantine

1 3-lb piece of breast of veal — this should preferably be almost square
salt and pepper
1 ½ lb good quality sausagemeat
6 tablespoons white wine
2 tablespoons chopped parsley
1 teaspoon chopped thyme
½ lb cooked ham
3 ¾ pints stock
1 onion
2 carrots

Remove all the bones from the veal, lay it out flat and season well with salt and pepper. Blend the sausagemeat with the wine and herbs, then spread this over the veal, leaving 1 in all the way round the edges. Cut the ham into thick strips and lay this down the middle. Roll up the meat and secure with string. Wrap the roll in cheesecloth and tie it up. Heat the stock in a large pan with the veal bones, the onion and carrots. When it is boiling, add the veal, lower the heat and simmer gently for 3 ½ hours. Take the pan off the heat and carefully take out the galantine. Remove the cheesecloth and put the galantine into a dish or pan about 1 in larger all round than itself. Boil the stock from the pan rapidly until it is reduced to about 2½ cups, then strain over the galantine. Put weights on top of the meat to press it down. Leave overnight until the meat is cold and the stock has formed a jelly all round it. Dip the container in hot water for about ½ minute, turn the galantine out onto a serving plate and garnish attractively.

Serves 8-10

Fish and shellfish

It is in the fish dishes, almost more than anywhere, that one can see the enormous difference between the cooking of northern and southern France. The dishes of the north tend to be made with the delicate white fish — sole, whiting, turbot — which are found in the northern waters and are often served in light, creamy sauces with a shellfish garnish. On the other hand the Mediterranean produces mullet, sea-bass, John Dory, octopus, and these are often served with vegetables — olives, zucchini, eggplant — which have been cooked in olive oil. As France has such a long coastline it is not surprising that fish plays an important part in French meals, but what is perhaps unexpected is that the French often rely on imported salt cod for their fish dishes. This is prized not only in France, but also in Spain and Italy, and many delicious dishes have been made from it, the most famous of all possibly being *brandade de morue* (see page 111). Salt cod can be obtained from some markets, but in recipes which call for salt cod you can always use fresh cod and add salt.

Court bouillon
Fish stock

A *court bouillon* is used for poaching fish, which can then either be served hot or cold. It is particularly used for fish, such as salmon, which are served cold; or as a basis for soups.

3¾ cups water
1¼ cups white wine

1 onion, finely chopped
2 shallots, finely chopped
1 carrot, finely chopped
1 *bouquet garni*
1 teaspoon salt
a few white peppercorns

Put all the ingredients into a saucepan. Cover, bring to the boil and simmer gently for about 40 minutes. Strain and use as required.
Makes about 5 cups

Poisson grillé au fenouil
Broiled fish with fennel

In this recipe dried fennel stalks are set alight and the fragrant smoke from them flavours the fish. Dried fennel stalks are packaged commercially in France, but you may prepare your own by cutting the narrow upper stalks, about 12 inches in length, from the fennel bulb and drying them thoroughly in a warm, dry place.

1 3 lb sea-bass, sea-bream, grey mullet, red mullet or mackerel
salt and pepper
4 tablespoons olive oil
about 6 dried fennel sticks

Season the fish, inside and out, with salt and pepper and brush all over with the olive oil. Place the fish on the grid of the broiler pan and put under a moderate flame for about 20 minutes, turning once. Remove from the heat and place the broiler pan on top of a heatproof surface. Put the fennel sticks into the broiler pan and light them; it is best to do this with a long taper. After about 2 minutes, very carefully turn the fish over so that the second side can be smoked. Serve as soon as possible.
Serves 4

Loup de mer farci au crabe
Baked sea-bass stuffed with crab

2 5-lb sea-bass, sea-bream or grey mullet
salt and pepper
3 medium-sized onions
6 tablespoons butter
2 sticks celery, finely chopped
1 teaspoon finely chopped fennel root
1 ⅔ cups fresh white breadcrumbs
6 oz fresh or canned crab meat
1 egg, beaten
1 ¼ cups white wine

Sprinkle the fish with salt and pepper inside and out. Finely chop one of the onions and fry in 2 tablespoons of the butter with the celery for about 10 minutes or until soft and golden brown. Stir in the fennel, breadcrumbs, crab meat and seasoning and bind together with the egg. Use this mixture to stuff the cavity of the fish and secure the opening with string, latticed between skewers. Place the fish in a large ovenproof dish. Thinly slice the remaining onions and sprinkle over the top of the fish. Pour over the wine, and bake the fish in a moderate oven (350°F) for 1 hour.
Serves 8

Brandade de morue
Creamed salt cod

This salt cod dish was traditionally served on Fridays, and is a specialty of the Languedoc.

1 lb salt cod
2 cloves garlic, crushed
¾ cup milk

¾ cup olive oil
freshly milled black pepper
To garnish:
bread
oil for frying

Soak the cod overnight in cold water. Drain and put into a saucepan with fresh cold water. Cover, bring gently to the boil, then drain. Remove and discard all the skin and bones, and flake the fish. Return to the saucepan with the garlic. Put the milk and olive oil into two separate saucepans and put these and the cod over a very low heat. Using a wooden spoon, very gradually beat in the milk and oil alternately, adding about a tablespoon at a time, until it has all been used. It is most important to keep on beating and to keep an even low heat. Season to taste with black pepper and serve the *brandade* warm, garnished with triangles of fried bread.
Serves 4-6

Morue brestoise
Salt cod with potatoes

1 lb salt cod
1 *bouquet garni*
4 tablespoons butter
2 large onions, chopped
3 leeks, chopped
1 tablespoon flour
⅔ cup milk
salt and pepper
2 lb potatoes
4 tablespoons dried breadcrumbs

Soak the cod overnight in cold water. Drain and put into a saucepan with fresh cold water to cover and a *bouquet garni*. Cover and simmer gently for 20 minutes or until the fish is tender. Melt half the butter in another saucepan and fry the onions and leeks

for about 10 minutes. Sprinkle in the flour and cook for about 1 minute, then gradually stir in ⅔ cup liquid from cooking the fish, and the milk. Bring to the boil, stirring all the time. Season to taste. Peel the potatoes and cut into slices about ¼ in thick. In a large, buttered, ovenproof dish, put about half the fish, then half the potatoes, then add the remainder of the cod and potatoes. Pour over the onion and leek sauce, then sprinkle with the breadcrumbs. Dot with the remaining butter and bake in a moderately hot oven (400°F) for about 45 minutes.
Serves 6

Cabillaud aux tomates
Cod with tomatoes

4 tablespoons butter
4 codfish steaks
salt and pepper
1 onion, chopped
1 clove garlic, crushed
½ lb tomatoes
½ lb mushrooms, sliced
5 tablespoons white wine
2 tablespoons chopped parsley

Melt the butter in a frying pan, season the fish with salt and pepper and cook gently in the butter for about 12 minutes, turning once. Remove from the pan, place on a heated serving dish and keep warm. Add the onion and garlic to the fat remaining in the pan and cook gently for about 10 minutes. Skin the tomatoes, cut them into quarters and remove the pips. Add the tomatoes and mushrooms to the pan and cook for a further 3 minutes, then stir in the wine and bring to the boil. Season, lower the heat and simmer gently for 5 minutes. Spoon the mixture over the fish and sprinkle with chopped parsley.
Serves 4

Filets de sole aux crevettes
Sole with prawns

1 lb prawns or shrimp
2 large or 4 small sole, filleted, bones reserved
1 *bouquet garni*
salt and pepper
2 cups water
⅓ cup white wine
¼ lb button mushrooms
3 tablespoons butter
5 tablespoons flour
⅔ cup light cream

Shell most of the prawns, reserving a few for garnishing. Put the shells, the fish bones, the *bouquet garni* and seasoning into a large saucepan. Add the water and bring slowly to the boil. Simmer for about 10 minutes. Strain the liquid off into another pan and add the wine. Roll the fillets of fish up and secure them with a toothpick. Poach the fish in the hot liquid for about 10 minutes, then remove with a slotted spoon and place on a heated serving dish.

Poach the sliced mushrooms in the stock for a further 5 minutes. Melt the butter in another pan, stir in the flour and cook for 2 minutes. Gradually stir in all the strained stock, then bring to the boil, stirring all the time. Add the prawns, mushrooms and cream and heat gently, without boiling. Taste and adjust the seasoning, then pour over the fillets of fish. Garnish with the remaining prawns.
Serves 4

Gratin de sardines aux tomates
Sardines with tomatoes

1 lb fresh sardines or young fresh herring, heads removed
salt and pepper

1 lb tomatoes
2 tablespoons olive oil
2 tablespoons butter
3 tablespoons fresh white breadcrumbs
1 tablespoon chopped parsley
1 clove garlic, crushed

Clean the fish and season with salt and pepper. Skin the tomatoes, cut into quarters, take out the seeds and discard. Quickly fry the tomato quarters in the oil for about 5 minutes, then place them in a lightly greased heatproof dish and season with salt and pepper. Add the butter to the frying pan, leave it to melt, then fry the fish for about 3 minutes on each side. Place the fish on top of the tomatoes in the dish. Mix the breadcrumbs with the parsley and garlic, then sprinkle over the fish in the dish. Spoon over them the butter from cooking the fish. Put under a hot broiler for 5 minutes or until the breadcrumbs are brown.
Serves 4-6 as an hors d'oeuvre or 2-3 as a main course

Sardines aux épinards
Sardines with spinach

1 lb fresh sardines or young fresh herring, heads removed
salt and pepper
2 lb fresh spinach or 2 pkgs frozen chopped spinach, cooked briefly and drained
4 tablespoons olive oil
1 large onion, finely chopped
2 cloves garlic, crushed
2 tablespoons fresh white breadcrumbs

Season the fish with salt and pepper. If using fresh spinach, wash, then cook in 2 tablespoons salted water until tender. Drain thoroughly and chop finely. Heat 2 tablespoons of the oil in a pan and fry the onion gently for about 5 minutes. Add the spin-

ach, garlic and seasoning and mix well. Turn into the bottom of a lightly greased ovenproof dish. Place the fish on top. Sprinkle with the breadcrumbs, then with the remaining olive oil. Bake in a moderately hot oven (375°F) for 20 minutes.
Serves 4-6 as an hors d'oeuvre or 2-3 as a main course

Maquereaux à la bretonne
Mackerel with shrimps

4 medium-sized mackerel, filleted
3 tablespoons flour
salt and pepper
6 tablespoons butter
1 onion, very finely chopped
4-6 oz peeled shrimps
2 tablespoons lemon juice
1 tablespoon chopped parsley
1 tablespoon chopped chives
2 teaspoons chopped fresh dill, if available

Lightly dust the mackerel fillets in flour seasoned with salt and pepper. Melt the butter in a large frying pan and gently fry the fish on both sides for about 5 minutes. Remove from the pan, place on a heated serving dish and keep warm. Add the very finely chopped onion to the pan and cook for about 5 minutes until golden brown. Add the remaining ingredients and heat well, then pour over the mackerel fillets. Serve as soon as possible.
Serves 4

Truite aux amandes
Trout with almonds

4 trout cleaned, with heads on
salt and pepper
6 tablespoons butter

½ cup flaked almonds
juice 1 small lemon

Season the trout with salt and pepper. Melt the butter in a frying
pan and fry the trout on each side for about 6 minutes, until
golden brown and cooked through. Remove the trout from the
pan, place on a heated serving dish and keep warm. Fry the
almonds in the butter remaining in the pan until golden. Add the
lemon juice, mix well and spoon over the fish.
Serves 4

Perche ou truite en papillotes
Perch or trout in a parcel

4 medium-sized perch or trout, cleaned and scaled
salt and pepper
4 tablespoons butter
1 small onion, very finely chopped
½ lb button mushrooms, finely chopped
2 tablespoons chopped parsley
4 tablespoons white wine

Season the fish with salt and pepper, and lay each fish on a
separate lightly buttered piece of foil. Melt the butter in a saucepan and fry the onion, mushrooms and parsley for about 8
minutes or until the onion is transparent. Divide this mixture
between the four fish and pour a tablespoonful of wine over each
one. Crimp the edges of the foil together so that the fish is completely enclosed and the juices cannot escape, then place the
parcels on a baking sheet. Bake in a moderately hot oven (375°F)
for 20 minutes. Arrange the fish on a serving dish and open out
the foil.
Serves 4

Filets de merlan à la meunière
Whiting fillets meunière

This is one of the simplest, yet most delicious ways of cooking fish. It is particularly suitable for white fish such as whiting and flounder, but is also good for others such as herring and trout.

4 medium-sized whiting, filleted and skinned
flour
salt and pepper
1 egg, lightly beaten
6 tablespoons butter
juice ½ lemon
1 tablespoon chopped parsley

Dip the fillets of fish first in flour seasoned with salt and pepper and then in the beaten egg. Heat 4 tablespoons of the butter in a frying pan, add the fish and cook gently on both sides for abut 3 minutes, turning once. Remove the fish from the pan, place on a heated serving dish and keep warm. Add the remaining butter to the pan and when foaming stir in the lemon juice and parsley. Bring to the boil, then spoon over the fish.
Serves 4

Merlans au four
Oven-baked whiting

4 whiting, filleted and skinned
salt and pepper
2 tablespoons butter
2 shallots, finely chopped
¼ lb mushrooms, sliced
1¼ cups dry white wine
1 tablespoon cornstarch
1 tablespoon tomato paste

2 tablespoons water
pinch sugar

Place the whiting in a greased ovenproof dish and season with salt and pepper. Melt the butter in a small saucepan and fry the shallots and mushrooms for about 2-3 minutes. Add the wine and boil, uncovered, for about 6 minutes. Blend the cornstarch with the tomato paste and water and stir this into the wine mixture with the sugar. Bring back to the boil, stirring all the time. Pour the sauce over the whiting in the dish. Cover and bake in a moderate oven (350°F) for about 15 minutes.
Serves 4

Merlans à la bretonne
Whiting with vegetables

Other fish such as haddock and flounder can be used for this dish in place of whiting.

4 whiting, filleted
salt and pepper
⅔ cup white wine
⅔ cup water
2 leeks
2 stalks celery
3 carrots
¼ lb mushrooms
1 tablespoon butter
1 tablespoon flour
⅔ cup light or heavy cream

Season the fish with salt and pepper and place in a fairly large, shallow fireproof dish. Add the wine and water. Slice the leeks,

celery, carrots and mushrooms very thinly and sprinkle over the fish. Cover and bake in a very moderate oven (325°F) for 40 minutes. Remove from the oven and place the fish on a serving plate. Blend the butter with the flour until it is a smooth paste. Bring the cooking liquid and vegetables to the boil on the top of the stove, and stir in the butter and flour a teaspoon at a time. Simmer for about 2 minutes after all the butter and flour has been incorporated, then stir in the cream. Heat gently, but do not allow the sauce to boil. Taste and adjust the seasoning, then pour over the fish and serve.
Serves 4

Harengs lyonnaise
Herrings Lyonnaise

4 herrings
2 tablespoons flour
salt and pepper
4 tablespoons butter
1 large onion, finely chopped
1 tablespoon white wine vinegar
2 tablespoons chopped parsley

Toss the herrings in the flour seasoned with salt and pepper. Heat the butter in a frying pan and fry the herrings for about 6 minutes on each side or until cooked. Remove from the pan, place on a heated serving dish and keep warm. Add the onion to the pan and cook gently for about 6 minutes or until golden. Add the vinegar, let it bubble for 1 minute, then pour over the herrings. Sprinkle the herrings liberally with the parsley and serve as soon as possible.
Serves 4

Harengs à la nantaise
Herrings with soft roe sauce

For this dish you need herrings with soft roes and if you ask your fish dealer he will be able to pick these out for you.

4 herrings
salt and pepper
4 tablespoons butter
1 teaspoon strong French mustard

Clean the herrings and season them with salt and pepper. Heat the butter in a frying pan and fry the herrings for about 6 minutes on each side or until they are cooked. Remove from the pan and place on a serving dish. Add the soft roes to the pan and fry for about 5 minutes, or until cooked. Sieve them into a clean pan, add the mustard and seasoning and heat gently. Turn this mixture into a small heated dish and serve separately with the herrings.
Serves 4

Rougets niçois
Red mullet with mushrooms and herbs

Red mullet are also known as 'the woodcock of the sea' since you can eat them whole. However, if you're not sure how old the fish are, you should prepare them in the normal way and remove their heads and tails. Use gray mullet if red is unavailable.

4 red mullet
2 tablespoons olive oil
salt and pepper

⅔ cup dry white wine
5 or 6 button mushrooms, finely chopped
1 small onion, finely chopped
1 shallot, finely chopped
2 tablespoons chopped parsley

Brush the mullet with the oil and season with salt and pepper. Place them in a shallow, ovenproof dish, add the wine and sprinkle with the mushrooms, onion, shallot and parsley. Cover the dish and bake in a moderately hot oven (400°F) for 20 minutes or until the fish are cooked.
Serves 4

Bouillabaisse
Mediterranean fish stew

It is impossible to make a genuine *bouillabaisse* away from the shores of the Mediterranean where there is such an enormous variety of fresh fish, but this is a simple recipe which nevertheless is very good.

1 lb cod fillet, skinned
1 red (or gray) mullet, boned
1 small mackerel, boned
½ lobster
1 leek, chopped
1 onion, chopped
2 tomatoes, skinned and chopped
2 cloves garlic, crushed
pinch of powdered saffron or ¼ teaspoon saffron sticks crushed and soaked in 2 tablespoons water
1 bay leaf
2 tablespoons chopped parsley
1 teaspoon salt
freshly milled black pepper
4 tablespoons olive oil

3¾ cups water
½ lb peeled shrimps

Cut the cod, mullet and mackerel into 1½-in pieces. Break off
the claws and legs of the lobster, and take out the meat from the
claws. Cut the body of the lobster into 1½-in pieces, cutting
through the shell.

Put the leek, onion, tomatoes, garlic, saffron, bay leaf,
parsley, salt and pepper into a large saucepan. Add the oil and
water, cover and bring to the boil. Lower the heat and simmer,
uncovered, for 10 minutes. Add all the fish, cover and simmer
for a further 10 minutes. Serve immediately.
Serves 6

Coquilles St-Michel
Scallops with cheese and cream

8 large (sea) scallops
1 small onion or shallot, chopped
1¼ cups white wine
2 tablespoons butter
2 tablespoons flour
½ cup + 2 tablespoons milk
2 tablespoons grated Parmesan cheese
salt and pepper
4 tablespoons heavy cream, lightly whipped

Wash the scallops thoroughly and put into a saucepan with the
onion or shallot and wine. Simmer gently until the scallops become opaque, about 10 minutes. Remove the scallops and onion
or shallot from the pan with a slotted spoon. Boil the liquid
rapidly until it is reduced to about 5 tablespoons.

Melt the butter in a saucepan, stir in the flour and cook for a
minute. Remove from the heat and gradually stir in the milk.
Return to the heat, and bring to the boil, stirring until thickened.
Stir in half the grated cheese and the wine in which the scallops
were cooked.

Chop the scallops and add to the sauce with the onion. Taste
and adjust the seasoning. Spoon the mixture into scallop shells or

ramekins. Add the cheese to the whipped cream and spread evenly over the scallops.

Put under the grill and wait until the cheese bubbles and is golden brown.

Serves 4

Coquilles St-Jacques à la provençale
Scallops with garlic butter

12 large (sea) scallops
½ cup butter
1 medium-sized onion, very finely chopped
salt and freshly milled black pepper
2 tablespoons chopped parsley
1 clove garlic, crushed
2 teaspoons lemon juice

Clean the scallops well and remove any grit. Chop each one roughly into 3 or 4 pieces. Heat 1 tablespoon of the butter in a pan and gently fry the onion for 5 minutes, add the scallops and seasoning and cook gently for about 10 minutes until they are quite opaque.

While the scallops are cooking, melt the remainder of the butter in a separate small pan, then add the parsley, garlic, lemon juice and seasoning. When cooked, turn the scallops into a small serving dish and spoon over the garlic butter.

Serves 3-4 as a main course, 6 as an hors d'oeuvre

Langoustines provençale
Scampi cooked in tomatoes

2 tablespoons olive oil
1 medium-sized onion, chopped
1 clove garlic, crushed
1 lb tomatoes

1 tablespoon dry white wine
1 tablespoon chopped parsley
salt and pepper
1 lb. cooked scampi or large shrimp

Heat the oil in a pan. Add the onion and garlic and cook gently
for about 10 minutes or until the onion is soft. Skin the tomatoes,
cut into quarters and remove the seeds. Add the tomatoes to the
pan with the wine, parsley and seasoning. Cover and cook for 10
minutes. Add the scampi to the pan and simmer gently for about
5 minutes. It is important not to overcook the shellfish or they
will become very tough.
Serves 4 as an hors d'oeuvre or 2 as a main course

Crabe niçoise
Crab with herbs and olives

1 large crab, about 4 lb
1 clove garlic, crushed
2 tablespoons chopped parsley
1 tablespoon chopped chives
3 black olives, finely chopped
4 tablespoons fresh white breadcrumbs
3 tablespoons olive oil
salt and freshly milled black pepper
cayenne pepper
2 tablespoons grated Parmesan cheese

Take all the meat out of the shell, body and claws of the crab and
put into a bowl with the garlic, parsley, chives, olives, three-
quarters of the breadcrumbs and the oil. Mix well and season to
taste with salt, black pepper and cayenne pepper. Either return
the mixture to the crab shell or place in a lightly greased ovenproof dish. Sprinkle with the remaining breadcrumbs and cheese
and bake in a moderately hot oven (400°F) for 20 minutes.
Serves 6-8 as an hors d'oeuvre or 3-4 as a main course

Moules marinière

4 quarts fresh mussels
4 tablespoons butter
4 shallots, chopped
few parsley stalks
1 sprig thyme
1 bay leaf
freshly milled black pepper
1¼ cups white wine
1 tablespoon flour
salt
2 tablespoons chopped parsley

Scrub the mussels with a scrubbing brush and remove all the traces of seaweed, mud and beard. Wash them in several changes of water and discard any which are badly cracked and any that do not close when sharply tapped: mussels which remain open are dead and should not be used. Drain the mussels in a colander.

Melt half the butter in a large pan and gently fry the shallots until they are soft, but not coloured. Add the herbs, pepper and wine and then the mussels. Cover the pan and cook quickly, shaking the pan constantly until the mussels open; this will take about 5 minutes. Lift the mussels out of the pan, using a draining spoon, and discard the empty half of each shell. Place the mussels in a heated serving dish and keep warm.

Boil the cooking liquor rapidly in an open pan until it is reduced by about half. Remove the herbs. Blend the remainder of the butter with the flour to a smooth paste. Drop this into the simmering stock, a teaspoon at a time and cook, stirring, until the stock is smooth and thickened. Pour over the mussels and sprinkle with the chopped parsley.
Serves 4-6

Moules au gratin
Mussels with garlic and breadcrumbs

4 quarts mussels
1 onion, chopped
few parsley stalks
1 sprig thyme
⅔ cup water
⅔ cup white wine or use an extra ⅔ cup water
½ cup butter
2 teaspoons lemon juice
2 cloves garlic, crushed
2 tablespoons chopped parsley
4 tablespoons fresh white breadcrumbs

Clean and prepare the mussels as for *moules marinière* (see above). Put the onion, parsley, thyme, water and wine, if using, into a large saucepan and bring to the boil. Add the mussels, cover with a tightly fitting lid and cook quickly, shaking the pan constantly. As soon as the mussels open, quickly remove from the heat.

Discard the empty half of each shell and place the rest in a shallow fireproof dish. If you do not have a large enough dish, you may have to do this in two lots. While the mussels are cooking, melt the butter in a pan over low heat. Remove from the heat and stir in the lemon juice, garlic and parsley. Spoon this over the mussels and sprinkle with the breadcrumbs. Put under a moderate broiler and cook for about 3 minutes or until golden brown.

Variations:
Add 6 tablespoons grated Parmesan cheese to the breadcrumbs and sprinkle the mussels with this mixture.

Reduce the liquid in which the mussels were cooked to ⅔ cup by rapid boiling. Remove from the heat, stir in ⅔ cup cream and strain this mixture into the dish before spooning the butter over.

Homard Thermidor
Lobster Thermidor

This is one of the classic lobster dishes, but the basic sauce mixture could be used just as well for crayfish, crab or large shrimp.

2 medium-sized cooked lobsters, about 2½ lb each
few drops olive oil
2 shallots, finely chopped
few parsley sprigs
1 sprig tarragon
few sprigs chervil
1¼ cups white wine
3 tablespoons butter
4 tablespoons flour
1¼ cups milk
2 teaspoons French mustard
4 tablespoons heavy cream
salt and pepper
4 tablespoons grated Parmesan cheese

Split the lobsters in half, remove the black intestinal vein and discard this together with the stomach. Take the flesh out of the shells and put on one side together with the meat from the claws. Reserve the lobster shells and polish these with the olive oil.

Put the shallots, parsley sprigs, tarragon and chervil into a saucepan with the wine and cook without a lid over a moderate heat until the wine is reduced to about 4 tablespoons. Melt the butter in another pan, stir in the flour and cook for about a minute. Gradually stir in the milk and bring to the boil, stirring all the time. Stir in the mustard, strained wine and cream and heat the sauce gently. Finally stir in the lobster flesh, heat gently, taste and season with salt and pepper. You may need to add a little more mustard, depending on the strength of the variety you have used. Spoon the lobster and sauce back into the lobster shells and sprinkle with cheese. Put under a hot grill and cook for a couple of minutes or until the cheese is golden brown.
Serves 4

Quenelles de brochet
Pike fish balls

Quenelles are traditionally made with pike but you can easily use another fish, such as whiting, instead. If you like *quenelles* but do not want to go to the bother of making them you can buy very good cans of them which you could serve with the shrimp sauce below.

2 lb pike
1 onion, chopped
2 stalks celery, chopped
1 carrot, chopped
1 *bouquet garni*
salt and pepper
5 cups water
pâte à choux made with ½ cup + 2 tablespoons flour
(see page 225)
good pinch grated nutmeg
about 4 tablespoons heavy cream

For the sauce:
4 tablespoons butter
¼ lb mushrooms, very finely chopped
4 tablespoons flour
½ cup + 2 tablespoons milk
½ lb small peeled shrimps
4 tablespoons heavy cream
salt and pepper

Remove all the bones and skin from the fish. Put these into a saucepan with the onion, celery, carrot, *bouquet garni*, seasoning and water. Cover and simmer gently for 30 minutes, then strain, reserving the liquid.

Grind the fish finely then either sieve it through a coarse sieve or pound it. Add to the *pâte à choux* with the nutmeg and seasoning. Cover the mixture and leave to chill in the refrigerator for at least 2 hours. Before cooking add sufficient cream to give a light mixture, but it should not be too sticky.

Heat the fish stock in a large open pan until it is just simmering. Drop teaspoonfuls of the *quenelle* mixture into the stock and poach them for about 10-15 minutes, turning once. Remove them from the pan with a slotted spoon and keep warm on a heated serving dish.

While the *quenelles* are cooking, start preparing the sauce. Melt the butter in a saucepan, add the mushrooms and cook gently for about 5 minutes. Stir in the flour and cook for a further minute, then remove from the heat and gradually stir in the milk. When all the *quenelles* are cooked, add 1¼ cups of the stock from cooking them to the sauce and then bring it to the boil, stirring all the time. Add the shrimps and cream, taste and adjust the seasoning, then pour this sauce over the *quenelles*.
Serves 4-6

Meat

The way in which meat, particularly beef, is butchered in France is rather different from the English and American methods, with the result that cuts of meat vary enormously. Although some London and New York butchers may sell Continental cuts, this is by no means common and I have therefore kept to cuts of meat with which readers will be familiar, even if they are not quite correct technically.

Wine is, of course, used extensively in French meat cookery, but by no means do all the recipes in this chapter use it, and in many of them it could be replaced with good stock for everyday use. You may also like to try replacing white wine in recipes with *dry* cider, which does not taste quite the same, but gives a very good result.

Filet de boeuf en croûte
Fillet of beef in puff pastry

1 2-lb fillet of beef
salt and freshly milled black pepper
4 tablespoons butter
1 clove garlic, crushed
½ lb mushrooms, finely chopped
2 tablespoons brandy
pâte feuilletée made with 2 cups flour (see page 225) or use a
14-oz packet frozen puff pastry, thawed
1 egg yolk
1 tablespoon water

Season the beef with salt and pepper. Heat the butter in a frying pan and fry the beef and garlic for about 15 minutes, turning the meat so that it becomes browned on all sides. Remove the beef from the pan and put on one side. Add the mushrooms to the pan and cook gently until soft. Remove from the heat and stir in the brandy. Roll the pastry out to a size large enough to completely envelop the meat. Put the beef into the centre of the pastry with the mushrooms and juices on top. Beat the egg yolk with the water and brush the edges of the pastry. Bring them together and seal well so that the meat is completely enclosed. Turn the meat over so that the seams are underneath and place on a baking sheet. Any pastry trimmings can be rolled out and cut into leaves for decoration. Brush all over the pastry with the remainder of the egg wash and bake in a hot oven (425°F) for 20 minutes, then lower the heat to (375°F) for a further 10-15 minutes or until the pastry is golden.
Serves 6-8

Variation: This recipe can also be used for veal. Ask your butcher to bone and roll a small roast from the leg, about 3 lb in weight. Dot the meat with half the butter and season with salt and pepper. Wrap loosely in foil and roast in a moderate oven (350°F) for 2 hours. Allow to cool. Fry the mushrooms in the remaining butter and then continue as for boeuf en croûte, above.

Romsteck à la crème
Steaks with cream sauce

4 club steaks, about ½ lb each
salt and pepper
4 tablespoons butter
1 tablespoon olive oil
2 tablespoons red wine vinegar
⅔ cup heavy cream

Season the steaks with salt and pepper. Heat the butter and oil in a frying pan and fry the steaks on both sides; the length of cooking time will depend on how well done you like your steaks but about 4 minutes on each side will give you a medium rare steak. Remove the steaks from the pan and place on a warm serving dish. Add the vinegar to the pan and quickly bring to the boil. Reduce the heat and stir in the cream. Heat gently without allowing the cream to boil, taste and adjust the seasoning then pour over the steaks.
Serves 4

Romsteck au poivre
Pepper steak

Ideally green peppercorns should be used here but black ones are quite adequate.

1 tablespoon peppercorns
4 small club or fillet steaks
salt
4 tablespoons butter
1 tablespoon oil
2 tablespoons brandy
⅔ cup heavy cream

Put the peppercorns between the folds of a clean tea towel and crush with a rolling pin. Sprinkle a little salt over both sides of each steak, then press in the crushed peppercorns.

Heat the butter and oil in a frying pan and fry the steaks on both sides until they are as cooked as you like; about 4 minutes on each side will give you a medium rare steak. Pour the brandy over them and ignite it. When the flames have died down, remove the steaks from the frying pan, place on a heated serving dish and keep warm. Stir the cream into the juices remaining in the pan and heat gently. Taste and adjust the seasoning and serve this sauce separately with the steaks.
Serves 4

Boeuf en daube
Beef in red wine with olives

There are many ways of preparing *boeuf en daube* and this is one of the simplest. Originally the beef was cooked in a closed earthenware pot (or *daubière*) which was buried completely in hot cinders and left alone to stew gently for a very long time.

4 onions, sliced
2 carrots, peeled and sliced
2 cloves garlic, crushed
1 bay leaf
1 sprig rosemary
3 sprigs parsley
2 cloves
salt and pepper
peeled zest ½ orange
1 tablespoon wine vinegar
2 cups red wine
2 lb lean chuck steak
2 strips fat bacon
4 tablespoons flour
1 cup green or black olives

Put two of the onions, the carrots, garlic, herbs, cloves, seasoning, orange zest, vinegar and wine into a shallow dish. Cut the beef into large cubes, about 1½ in square, add to the wine mixture and leave to marinate for about 24 hours. Drain the meat from the marinade. Chop the bacon and put into a fireproof casserole. Heat gently until the fat runs, then increase the heat and add the meat and remaining onions. Cook for about 10 minutes, stirring until the meat is browned on all sides. Add the flour and cook until lightly browned, then stir in the strained marinade and bring to the boil. Cover and put into a very slow oven (300°F) for about 4 hours. Pit the olives and add them to the pan halfway through cooking.
Serves 6

Boeuf à la bourguignonne
Beef with wine and onions

1 ½ lb chuck steak
2 tablespoons lard or bacon fat
1 6 oz piece lean bacon, chopped
2 tablespoons flour
1 ¼ cups stock
⅔ cup Burgundy wine
1 *bouquet garni*
salt and freshly milled black pepper
8 to 12 small white onions, peeled

Cut the steak into 1 ½ in cubes. Melt the lard or bacon fat in a pan and fry the bacon for a few minutes until it begins to brown. Remove from the pan with a slotted spoon and place in an oven-proof casserole. Add the steak to the fat remaining in the pan and fry on all sides until the meat is browned. Remove from the pan and add to the bacon in the casserole. Pour off all but 2 tablespoons of the fat in the pan and stir in the flour. Cook over low heat until the flour is golden brown, then gradually stir in the stock and wine. Bring to the boil, stirring all the time, add the *bouquet garni* and season with salt and pepper. Pour over the meat in the casserole, cover and cook in a very moderate oven (325°F) for 1 ½ hours. Add the onions to the meat, then cook for a further hour or until the meat is quite tender.
Serves 4-6

Boeuf à la mode de Caen
Beef with vegetables and cider

This is a marvelous dish which you can put into the oven and then forget about. It is typical of many other French recipes for dishes which used to be cooked very slowly in the baker's oven, as it cooled down. The casserole should, in fact, be hermetically sealed with flour and water paste, and if the lid of your casserole does not fit very tightly, you may prefer to do this rather than use just foil and the lid.

1 calf's foot, split
2 tablespoons butter
2 lb good braising steak
2 tablespoons Calvados
5 cups cider
a few beef bones
1 lb small white onions, peeled
1 lb small carrots
2 cloves garlic, crushed
1 *bouquet garni*
salt and freshly milled black pepper
2 teaspoons French mustard

Put the calf's foot into a pan of cold water, bring to the boil and cook for 5 minutes, then drain. Heat the butter in a large, fire-proof casserole. Add the beef and cook quickly on all sides to seal it. Pour the Calvados over the beef and flame it. When the flames have died down, add the cider, and remaining ingredients, including the calf's foot. Cover the casserole, first with a double layer of foil and then a lid. Put into a very slow oven (275°F) and cook for 4 hours. Remove the calf's foot from the pan, chop the meat coarsely and place on a heated serving dish with the beef, carrots and onions. Remove and discard the bones and *bouquet garni*. Skim off the fat from the liquid, and boil the liquid rapidly in an open pan until it is reduced to about half. Pour into a sauce-boat and serve with the meat and vegetables.
Serves 6-8

Boeuf à la mode
Casseroled beef

1 4-lb roast of rolled round of beef
2 large carrots, sliced
1 large onion, chopped
1-2 cloves garlic, crushed
1 *bouquet garni*

6 peppercorns
1 teaspoon ground mixed spice (or ¼ teaspoon each mace,
clove, cinnamon, allspice)
2½ cups red wine
½ lb pork fat
5 cups beef stock
1 calf's foot or 2 pig's feet, split in half

Put the meat into a large bowl with the carrots, onion, garlic,
bouquet garni, peppercorns, mixed spice and red wine. Leave for
at least 12 hours to marinate, turning from time to time. Remove
the meat from the marinade and dry. Cut the pork into small
cubes and fry in a fireproof casserole over a low heat to begin
with so that the fat runs out. Increase the heat, add the meat and
quickly brown it on all sides. Remove the cubes of pork and pour
off any excess fat. Add the marinade and the beef stock. Put the
calf's foot or pig's feet into a pan of cold water, bring to the boil
and cook for 5 minutes. Drain, then add to the beef. Cover and
cook in a slow oven (325°F) for 3½ hours. Take the casserole out
of the oven, remove the meat, place on a heated serving dish and
keep warm. Boil the liquid in the casserole rapidly, uncovered,
until it is reduced to about 2½ cups. Strain into a sauceboat and
serve with the meat.
Serves 6-8

Pot-au-feu

A true French *pot-au-feu* consists of two separate parts — the
boiled beef and vegetables which are served at one meal and the
stock in which they were cooked which is used for *consommé* or
other soups and sauces which require a good stock with plenty of
flavour. While you can make a good *consommé* from beef bone
stock (see page 26) a very much better one will be obtained from
using the liquid from a *pot-au-feu*. It is also an excellent way of
using some of the cheaper cuts of beef, such as shin brisket,

and short ribs and, cooked in this way, these cuts are also excellent cold. You can, if you prefer, use a smaller quantity of beef, say about 2 lb and add a small chicken as well, or use about 3 lb beef and an oxtail.

4-lb piece of beef (see above)
a few chicken giblets (if available)
10 cups water
4 large carrots
4 large leeks
2 large onions
1 turnip
2 stalks celery
1 tablespoon salt
1 *bouquet garni*
1 beef marrow bone, chopped

Put the beef and chicken giblets, if using, into a large pan with the water. Slowly bring to simmering point and leave, uncovered, for about 15 minutes, skimming off all the grey scum. Peel or clean and roughly chop all the vegetables and add them to the pot with the salt and *bouquet garni*. Cover the pan and simmer gently for about 3½ hours. Wrap the pieces of marrow bone tightly in cheesecloth and tie with string. Add to the pan and continue cooking for a further 30 minutes. Serve the meat surrounded by the vegetables, and have a little of the cooking liquor separately in a sauceboat.
Serves 8-12

Alouettes sans têtes
Beef olives

For this recipe you need thin slices of beef round; your butcher will cut these for you, as it is much easier for him to slice the meat thinly off a large piece, than for you to try to cut up a small piece yourself. The literal translation of '*alouettes sans têtes*' is 'larks without heads'!

8 slices of beef round (see above)
½ cup ham, finely chopped
1 clove garlic, crushed
2 tablespoons chopped parsley
3 tablespoons fresh white breadcrumbs
grated zest 1 small lemon
salt and pepper
pinch grated nutmeg
1 onion, chopped
1 carrot, chopped
1 stalk celery, chopped
2 strips lean bacon, chopped
⅔ cup red wine
1 ¼ cups stock
1 teaspoon tomato paste
1 *bouquet garni*

Put the meat between two pieces of wax paper and beat it out until very thin. Mix the ham, garlic, 1 tablespoon of the parsley, the breadcrumbs, lemon zest, seasoning and nutmeg together. Divide the stuffing between the slices of beef, turn in the sides of the meat, and roll up to enclose the stuffing completely. Secure with thread. Put the onion, carrot, celery and bacon in the bottom of an ovenproof casserole. Put in the beef rolls, then pour over the wine and stock, mixed with the tomato paste. Add the *bouquet garni*, cover the casserole and cook in a very moderate oven (325°F) for 2 hours or until the meat is very tender. Remove the meat from the casserole, take off the string and arrange in a heated serving dish. Strain the juices from cooking the meat into a saucepan and boil quickly for a few minutes to reduce it, then pour over the meat. Sprinkle with the parsley before serving.
Serves 4

Queue de boeuf aux olives noires
Oxtail with black olives

1 large or 2 smaller oxtails cut in serving pieces
2 tablespoons olive oil
3 tablespoons brandy
¾ cup white wine
1 ¼ cups stock or water
salt and pepper
1 *bouquet garni*
1 ½ cups black olives, pitted
2 tablespoons butter
4 tablespoons flour
2 tablespoons chopped parsley

Put the oxtails into a bowl of cold water and leave for 2 hours. Drain and dry well on paper towels. Heat the oil in a fireproof casserole and fry the meat for about 10 minutes until golden brown all over. Pour the brandy over and ignite. When the flames have died down, add the wine and boil for about 5 minutes until the wine has reduced by half, then add the stock or water, seasoning and *bouquet garni*. Cover the casserole and put into a very slow oven (300°F) and cook for 4 hours, stirring in the olives one hour before the end of cooking.

Take the casserole out of the oven, remove the pieces of oxtail, place them on a heated serving dish and keep warm. Skim off all the excess fat from the juices and place the casserole over a moderate heat on top of the stove. Blend the butter with the flour to a smooth paste and gradually stir into the juices, a teaspoon at a time. Taste the sauce and adjust the seasoning. Pour over the oxtail and sprinkle with the parsley before serving.
Serves 4

Tourte morvandelle
Beef and sausage pie

pâte brisée made with 3 cups flour (see page 223)
1 tablespoon butter
2 medium-sized onions, very finely chopped
1 clove garlic, crushed
1 lb lean ground beef
1 lb good quality sausagemeat
salt and freshly milled black pepper
2 teaspoons chopped tarragon
2 egg yolks
1 tablespoon water

Roll out two-thirds of the pastry and use it to line a 9-in square or round pan, about 3 in deep. Melt the butter in a pan and fry the onions and garlic very gently for about 5 minutes. Turn into a bowl and add the beef, sausagemeat, seasoning and tarragon. Mix well and bind together with all but 1 tablespoon of the egg yolks. Turn this mixture into the pastry-lined pan and spread it out evenly. Mix the remainder of the egg yolk with the water and brush this round the edges of the pastry in the pan. Roll out the remaining pastry and lay over the meat. Seal the edges of the pastry well and trim off any excess. This can be rolled out and made into pastry leaves for decoration. Brush all over the top of the pie with the remaining egg and bake in a moderately hot oven (400°F) for 20 minutes, then lower the heat to moderate (350°F) for a further 40 minutes.
Serves 6-8

Langue de boeuf au gratin
Beef tongue with wine sauce

This is a very simple, quickly made dish. You can use bought cooked tongue; alternatively it is an ideal way of using up part of a whole tongue you have cooked yourself and of which you are getting rather bored.

4 slices beef tongue, about ¼ in thick
6 tablespoons butter
1 large onion, finely chopped
5 tablespoons flour
2 cups beef stock, or stock from cooking the tongue and
⅔ cup white wine, or use all stock
salt and pepper

Lay the slices of tongue in a well buttered ovenproof dish. Melt 4 tablespoons of the butter in a pan and fry the onion for about 10 minutes, stir in the flour and cook for a further 2 minutes. Remove from the heat and gradually stir in the stock and the wine, if used. Return to the heat and bring to the boil, stirring all the time. Season to taste with salt and pepper. Pour over the slices of tongue. Dot with the remaining butter and brown in a hot oven (425°F) for about 10 minutes.
Serves 4

Escalopes de veau à la savoyarde
Veal escalopes with vermouth

In the capital of the Savoie, Chambéry, they produce an excellent dry white vermouth.

4 escalopes of veal
salt and pepper
1 tablespoon lemon juice
4 tablespoons butter
5 tablespoons dry white vermouth
⅔ cup heavy cream

Ask your butcher to beat out the meat until it is very thin, or do this yourself by placing it between two sheets of wax paper and beating with a rolling pin or mallet. Season the meat with salt, pepper and lemon juice. Heat the butter in a frying pan and

fry the escalopes on both sides until they are beginning to brown. Add the vermouth and bring to the boil, then stir in the cream and cook gently for a few minutes until the sauce begins to thicken. Serve at once.
Serves 4

Carré de veau au Chablis
Roast veal with Chablis sauce

2½ lb loin or best end of veal, boned and rolled, bones
chopped and reserved
2 tablespoons butter
3 onions, quartered
4 carrots, chopped
1 tomato, quartered
1 sprig thyme
1 small bay leaf
1 clove garlic
salt and pepper
⅔ cup veal stock
1¼ cups Chablis, or other dry white wine

Heat the butter in a fireproof casserole and gently fry the onions, carrots, tomato, thyme, bay leaf and garlic for about 10 minutes. Season with salt and pepper, add the veal bones, then the meat and the veal stock. Cover the casserole and put into a very slow oven (300°F) for 2½ hours, basting from time to time. Remove the meat from the pan, place on a heated serving dish and keep warm. Add the Chablis to the casserole, bring to the boil on top of the stove and boil rapidly until it is reduced by half. Strain into a sauceboat and serve this sauce separately with the veal.
Serves 6

Paupiettes de veau
Veal birds

4 large scallops of veal
½ lb ground lean pork
2 onions, finely chopped
2 tablespoons fresh white breadcrumbs
1 tablespoon chopped parsley
salt and pepper
4 strips lean bacon
2 tablespoons butter
1 tablespoon oil
4 carrots, chopped
2 stalks celery, chopped
4 tablespoons flour
⅔ cup white wine
1¼ cups chicken or veal stock
1 *bouquet garni*

Beat out the veal scallops until they are very thin, or ask your butcher to do this for you. Mix together the pork, one of the onions, the breadcrumbs, parsley and seasoning. Lay the scallops out on a board and divide the pork mixture between them. Roll them up tightly, turning in the sides of the meat to make a neat parcel. Wrap a bacon strip round each parcel and secure the parcels with string.

Heat the butter and oil in a pan and gently fry the carrots, onion and celery for 5 minutes. Stir in the flour and cook for 2 minutes. Gradually stir in the wine and stock and bring to the boil, stirring all the time. Add the veal rolls, *bouquet garni* and seasoning. Cover and simmer gently for 1 hour. Remove the string and the bacon from the veal rolls, then return them to the sauce before serving.

Serves 4

Grenadins de veau Corbigny
Veal in cream sauce

4 slices of veal, about ¼ in thick, cut from the less tender
part of the leg
1 ½ oz pork fat
1 large onion, chopped
2 tablespoons butter
1 tablespoon oil
⅔ cup veal stock
⅔ cup white wine
¼ lb button mushrooms
1 tablespoon flour
⅔ cup heavy cream
salt and pepper

Using a larding needle, lard the slices of veal with the pork fat,
cut into very thin pieces. If you do not have a larding needle, you
can make small holes right through the meat with a skewer and
thread thin pieces of pork through these holes. Heat 1 tablespoon
of the butter and the oil in a fireproof casserole and fry the onion
for about 5 minutes. Increase the heat, add the veal to the pan
and fry quickly on both sides until just browned. Add the veal
stock and wine, and bring just to the boil. Place the dish in a very
moderate oven (325°F) and cook for about 1 hour or until the
veal is just tender. Remove the slices of veal and place on a
serving dish. Add the mushrooms to the liquid in the pan, and
blend the remaining butter with the flour. Bring the liquid to the
boil, on top of the stove, and stir in the blended butter and flour a
teaspoon at a time, stirring well. Simmer for about 2 minutes
after all the butter and flour has been incorporated, then stir in
the cream. Heat gently, but do not allow the sauce to boil, taste
and adjust the seasoning, then pour over the veal.
Serves 4

Sauté de veau chasseur
Veal with tomatoes and mushrooms

1 ½ lb stewing veal
2 tablespoons butter
1 tablespoon olive oil
4 shallots, chopped
1 clove garlic, crushed
4 tomatoes
4 tablespoons flour
⅔ cup white wine
1 ½ cups stock
salt and freshly milled black pepper
½ lb button mushrooms
¼ cup black olives

Cut the meat into 1-in cubes. Heat the butter and oil in a pan and fry the shallots, garlic and meat together for about 10 minutes. Skin the tomatoes, cut into quarters and remove the seeds. Add to the pan and cook for a further 5 minutes. Stir in the flour and cook for 2 minutes, then add the wine and stock and bring to the boil, stirring all the time. Season with salt and pepper. Cover the pan and simmer gently for 30 minutes. Fifteen minutes before the end of cooking add the mushrooms and olives.
Serves 4

Blanquette de veau
Veal casserole

1 ½ lb good stewing veal
4 tablespoons butter
½ lb small white onions, peeled
1 tablespoon oil
½ cup flour
3 ¾ cups veal stock
1 *bouquet garni*

6 white peppercorns
¼ lb button mushrooms, caps and stems separated
2 teaspoons lemon juice
⅔ cup cream
salt and pepper
To garnish:
8 strips bacon
2 slices white bread
2 tablespoons oil

Cut the meat into 1-in cubes. Heat the butter in a saucepan, add the meat and fry until it is just white, but do not allow it to brown. Remove the meat from the pan with a slotted spoon and put on one side. Add the onions and oil to the pan and cook these for 4-5 minutes, then remove from the pan. Add the flour to the fat remaining in the pan. Stir well and cook for about 2 minutes, remove from the heat and stir in the stock. Return to the heat and bring to the boil, stirring all the time until thickened. Add the *bouquet garni*, peppercorns and mushroom stems, cover and simmer gently for 30 minutes. Strain the sauce into a clean saucepan, replace the veal, onions and mushroom caps, cover and simmer gently for about 1 hour or until the meat is tender. Just before serving, stir in the lemon juice and cream and heat gently, but do not allow to boil. Check the seasoning. Turn into a serving dish and garnish with bacon rolls and fried bread croutons. To prepare the garnish, cut any rind off the bacon and roll the strips up neatly. Secure each with a toothpick and broil until golden brown. Cut the crusts off the bread and cut each slice into 8 triangles. Fry these in hot oil until golden brown.
Serves 4

Poitrine de veau farcie aux olives
Stuffed breast of veal with olives

This dish is excellent served hot or cold.

4 lb breast of veal boned, bones reserved
1 thick slice bread
milk
¼ lb lean pork, ground
⅔ cup black olives, pitted and roughly chopped
2 tablespoons chopped parsley
1 clove garlic, crushed
1 teaspoon finely chopped basil
¼ teaspoon grated nutmeg
salt and pepper
1 egg, beaten
2 tablespoons olive oil
1 onion, chopped
2 tomatoes, skinned and chopped
1¼ cups stock

Cut the crusts off the bread, put it into a little milk to soak for a few minutes, then wring completely dry. Put into a bowl with the pork, olives, parsley, garlic, basil, nutmeg and seasoning. Bind with the lightly beaten egg. Lay the meat out, with the skin side underneath, and spread over the stuffing. Roll up and tie securely with string.

Heat the oil in a large fireproof casserole, add the onion and cook for 5 minutes; add the meat and cook until golden brown all over. Then add the tomatoes and bones from the meat together with the stock and seasoning. Cover the casserole and put into a very slow oven, (300°F) for 3½ hours. Remove the meat and place on a serving dish. Skim off all the fat from the juices and strain into a sauceboat.
Serves 6-8

Sweetbreads are the pancreatic and thyroid glands of the animal and the most commonly used ones are those of lamb and veal. Sweetbreads, like other offal, are highly nutritious and can be cooked in a variety of ways, but before being cooked they should always be blanched in boiling water as in the recipes below.

Ris de veau à la crème et au jambon
Veal sweetbreads with cream and ham

Lamb's sweetbreads can be used instead of veal ones in this recipe. The dish can either be served on its own, or be used as a filling for *vol-au-vent* cases.

1 lb veal or lamb's sweetbreads
salt
2 tablespoons vinegar
3 tablespoons butter
1 small onion, very finely chopped
4 tablespoons flour
1 ¼ cups white wine
¼ lb button mushrooms, sliced
¼ lb ham, cut into ½-in cubes
1 teaspoon French mustard
⅔ cup cream

Soak the sweetbreads for at least 1 hour in cold water. Drain, put into a saucepan with fresh cold water, ½ teaspoon salt and the vinegar, and bring to the boil. Simmer lamb's sweetbreads for 20 minutes and veal sweetbreads for 30 minutes. Strain and place under running cold water. Remove any thick tissue, fat, blood-vessels and skin, and cut veal sweetbreads into 1½-in pieces. Melt the butter in a saucepan. Add the onion and fry gently for 5 minutes. Stir in the flour and cook for a minute, then gradually stir in the wine and bring to the boil, stirring all the time. Add the sweetbreads, mushrooms, ham, mustard and seasoning. Cover and simmer gently for 20 minutes. Stir in the cream and heat gently for a further 5 minutes, without boiling.
Serves 4

Ris de veau aux herbes
Sweetbreads with herbs

1 lb veal sweetbreads, or use lamb's sweetbreads
4 tablespoons butter
3 tablespoons chopped parsley
4 shallots, very finely chopped
2 cloves garlic, crushed
¼ lb mushrooms, finely chopped
4 tablespoons flour
2½ cups white wine
salt and pepper
4 strips lean bacon
1 *bouquet garni*

Soak the sweetbreads for at least 1 hour in cold water. Drain, put into a saucepan with fresh cold water, bring slowly to the boil, then boil for 1 minute. Strain and place under running cold water. Remove any thick tissue, fat, blood-vessels and skin.

Melt the butter in a saucepan, add 2 tablespoons of the parsley, the shallots, garlic and mushrooms, and cook gently for a few minutes. Stir in the flour and cook for a further minute, then gradually stir in the wine. Bring to the boil, stirring all the time until the mixture bubbles and thickens. Season and simmer gently for 10 minutes. Cut any rind off the bacon, lay on a board and stretch with the back of a knife. If using veal sweetbreads, cut into 1-in pieces; if using lamb's sweetbreads, leave whole. Wrap the bacon round the sweetbreads and secure with tooth-picks. Add to the wine sauce with the *bouquet garni*, cover and simmer for 45 minutes. Carefully remove the sweetbreads from the pan and place on a heated serving dish. Remove and discard the *bouquet garni*. Boil the sauce fairly rapidly until it is reduced to about 2 cups, then pour over the sweetbreads and sprinkle with the remaining parsley.

Serves 4

Rognons de veau aux raisins
Veal kidneys with grapes

2 veal kidneys or use about 12 lamb's kidneys
2 tablespoons butter
1 tablespoon tomato paste
1 tablespoon flour
1¼ cups dry white wine
salt and pepper
½ lb white grapes

Cut the kidneys into small pieces, removing the cores. Melt the butter in a pan and fry the kidneys for 5 minutes. Add the tomato paste and the flour, then gradually stir in the wine. Season with salt and pepper. Cover the pan and cook gently for about 10 minutes. Cut the grapes in half and remove the seeds. Add them to the pan and cook for a further 3 minutes.
Serves 4

Longe d'agneau à l'orléanaise
Roast loin of lamb

This recipe uses both the vinegar and the mustard which have made Orléans so well known gastronomically.

4 lb loin of lamb
salt and pepper
2 tablespoons French mustard, preferably Orléans mustard
2 tablespoons butter
1 tablespoon wine vinegar, preferably Orléans vinegar
⅔ cup white wine; this should be a medium dry Loire
wine, but you can use whatever you have available

Season the lamb well with salt and pepper, then spread all over with the mustard. Put into a roasting pan and dot with the butter. Roast in a moderately hot oven (375°F) for 2 hours. Baste the meat from time to time during cooking. When the meat is cooked, remove it to a serving plate and keep warm. Skim all the fat off the juices in the roasting pan, then place the pan on top of the stove. Add the vinegar and wine and simmer gently for about 5 minutes. Taste and adjust the seasoning and serve this sauce with the lamb.

Serves 6-8

Gigot d'agneau en croûte
Roast leg of lamb in pastry case

1 4 lb leg of lamb, boned
4 lamb's kidneys
6 tablespoons butter
1 clove garlic, crushed
salt and pepper
pâte feuilletée made with 3 cups flour (see page 225) or use a 14-oz and a 7½-oz packet of frozen puff pastry, thawed
1 egg yolk
1 tablespoon water

Cut the kidneys in half and remove the cores. Melt 2 tablespoons of the butter in a frying pan and fry the kidneys and garlic until tender. Season with salt and pepper and place the kidney mixture in the cavity left by the bone. Tie the roast securely with fine string, place in a roasting pan and rub all over with the remainder of the butter. Season with salt and pepper. Roast in a moderately hot oven (400°F) for 1¼ hours. Remove from the oven and allow to cool.

Roll out the pastry to a size large enough to envelop the meat. Remove the string from the lamb and place the meat in the centre of the pastry. Beat the egg yolk with water and brush the edges of the pastry. Bring the edges of the pastry together and seal well so that the meat is completely enclosed. Turn the meat over so that the seams are underneath and place on a baking sheet. Any

pastry trimmings can be rolled out and cut into leaves to decorate the top of the pastry. Brush all over the pastry with the remainder of the egg wash and bake in a hot oven (425°F) for 20 minutes, then lower the heat to 375°F) and bake for a further 25 minutes. If the pastry is becoming too brown, cover with foil so that it does not burn.
Serves 8

Gigot aux pommes Anna
Roast leg of lamb with potatoes

2 lb potatoes
4 tablespoons butter
salt and pepper
1-2 cloves garlic
1 3 lb leg of lamb

Peel the potatoes and cut into ½-in slices. Spread these potatoes over the bottom of a roasting pan or large ovenproof dish. Dot with most of the butter and season with salt and pepper. Cut the garlic into thin slivers and make small cuts in the fat of the lamb; insert the garlic slivers into the cuts, then spread the remainder of the butter over the lamb. Season with salt and pepper. Place the meat on top of the potatoes and roast in a moderately hot oven (375°) for 1½ hours.
Serves 6

Gigot provençale
Leg of lamb Provençale

This is an excellent way of cooking rather older lamb or young mutton. In Provence the joint is generally served with hot *ratatouille* (see page 62).

1 4-5 lb leg of lamb, boned
¾ lb salt pork

1 large slice bread
little milk
1 tablespoon chopped parsley
1 tablespoon chopped chives
3 cloves garlic, crushed
salt and pepper
1 egg yolk
4 tablespoons olive oil
1 onion, chopped
4 carrots, chopped
2 turnips, chopped
1 stalk celery
1¼ cups white wine
⅔ cup water
1 *bouquet garni*

Put the pork into a saucepan of cold water and leave for at least 4 hours, then drain, remove any skin and bones, and grind finely. Cut the crusts off the bread, soak in a little milk, then wring completely dry. Put the ground pork into a bowl with the bread, parsley, chives, garlic and seasoning and bind with egg yolk. Use this mixture to stuff the lamb, then tie the meat up with string. Heat the oil in a fireproof casserole and brown the meat on all sides, then remove from the pan. Add the onion, carrots, turnips and celery and cook until golden brown, then add the wine. Replace the meat and cook uncovered over a moderate heat until the wine is reduced to about 2 tablespoons, then add the water and *bouquet garni*. Put the casserole into a very moderate oven (325°F) and cook for 3-3½ hours, basting once or twice during cooking.
Serves 8-12

Épaule d'agneau aux noix
Shoulder of lamb stuffed with walnuts

1 3 lb shoulder of lamb, boned
4 tablespoons butter
1 small onion, very finely chopped
½ lb good sausagemeat
1 cup shelled walnuts, very finely chopped or ground
2 tablespoons chopped parsley
½ teaspoon chopped rosemary
grated zest 1 small orange
salt and freshly milled black pepper
1 egg, lightly beaten

Melt 2 tablespoons of the butter in a small pan and fry the onion for 5 minutes. Mix with the sausagemeat, walnuts, parsley, rosemary, orange zest and seasoning, and bind together with the beaten egg. Lay the meat out on a board and fill the cavity left by the bone with the stuffing. Using coarse thread or fine string, sew up the meat, then tie in two or three places with string. Spread the meat with the remaining butter and season with salt and pepper. Place on the rack of a roasting pan and roast in a hot oven (425°F) for 20 minutes, then lower the heat to moderately hot (375°F) for a further 1 hour 10 minutes. Baste the meat with the fat and juices from time to time during cooking.
Serves 6

Carbonnade nîmoise
Lamb with potatoes and carrots

This is a traditional dish from Nîmes in the Languedoc.

2 thick slices of lamb cut from the leg, about ⅓ in thick
¼ lb fat bacon
2 cloves garlic

2 tablespoons olive oil
2 lb potatoes
1 lb carrots
1 sprig thyme or marjoram
salt and pepper
¾ cup stock

Make small holes in the meat with the point of a skewer. Cut the bacon into thin strips and the garlic into fine slivers. Push some of the strips of bacon and garlic into the holes in the meat. If you have a larding needle, use this for the bacon. Place the meat in a casserole with the remaining bacon and garlic and the oil. Peel the potatoes and cut into 2-in squares, peel and roughly chop the carrots. Add these to the pan with the herbs and seasoning and pour over the stock. Put the casserole, uncovered, into a hot oven (425°F) for 20 minutes, then cover and cook in a very slow oven (300°F) for 3½-4 hours, by which time the meat will be very tender and the fat and stock will have been absorbed by the vegetables.
Serves 4

Côtelettes d'agneau en cuirasses
Lamb cutlets in pastry cases

6 large lamb cutlets
4 tablespoons butter
salt and pepper
2 tomatoes
6 oz mushrooms, very finely chopped
⅔ cup cooked ham, very finely chopped
1 tablespoon chopped parsley
pâte feuilletée made with 2 cups flour (see page 225) or use a 14-oz packet frozen puff pastry, thawed
1 egg yolk
2 tablespoons water

Dot the cutlets with 2 tablespoons of the butter, season with salt

and pepper and broil on both sides until tender. Skin the tomatoes, cut into quarters, remove the seeds and chop the flesh finely. Put into a bowl with the mushrooms, ham, parsley and seasoning. Melt the remaining butter, add to the mixture and blend well. Roll out the pastry and cut out 6 rectangles large enough to cover the cutlets completely. Put a spoonful of the ham mixture on each piece of pastry and place a cutlet on top. Top with another spoonful of ham mixture. Beat the egg yolk with the water and use to brush the edges of the pastry. Fold the pastry over and seal the edges so that each cutlet is completely enclosed. Place the cutlets, with the seams underneath, on a baking sheet. Any trimmings left from the pastry can be rolled out and cut into leaves for decoration. Brush all over the pastry with beaten egg and bake in a hot oven (425°F) for about 20 minutes or until golden brown.
Serves 6

Collier de mouton à la Bayonne
Lamb and vegetable casserole

2 lb middle neck of lamb
2 onions, quartered
2 large carrots, sliced
4 small turnips, peeled
¼ lb button mushrooms
1 bay leaf
1 tablespoon lemon juice
salt and pepper
5 cups stock or water
3 tablespoons butter
5 tablespoons flour
⅔ cup light cream
1 tablespoon chopped parsley

Ask the butcher to chop the lamb for you. Put into a pan with the onions, carrots, turnips, mushrooms, bay leaf, lemon juice, seasoning and stock or water. Bring to the boil, cover and simmer for 1½ hours or until the lamb is tender.

Remove the lamb and vegetables from the liquid with a slotted spoon, place in a deep, pre-heated serving dish and keep warm. Boil the cooking liquor rapidly until it is reduced to 2½ cups. Mix the butter with the flour to a smooth paste. Add this to the boiling liquor, a teaspoon at a time, stirring well between each additon; allow to cook for 2 minutes or until thickened. Reduce the heat, stir in the cream and heat gently without allowing it to boil. Taste and adjust the seasoning, then pour the sauce over the meat and vegetables and sprinkle with chopped parsley.
Serves 4

Variation: In Normandy a dish very similar to this is prepared, but the water is replaced by dry cider, and a couple of crushed cloves of garlic are also added.

Haricot de mouton
Mutton with haricot beans

This is a good, economical dish and the haricot beans soak up most of the fat from the lamb or mutton.

2 cups haricot (dried white) beans
salt
2 tablespoons butter
2 large onions, chopped
2 cloves garlic, crushed
1 ½ lb lean stewing lamb or mutton
2 cups stock
1 *bouquet garni*
1 sprig thyme
freshly milled black pepper

Soak the beans overnight in cold water. Drain, cover with fresh cold water and a little salt and bring to the boil. Cover and simmer gently for 30 minutes. Melt the butter in a large pan, add the onions and garlic and fry for 5 minutes. Chop the lamb into

1-in pieces, add to the onions and fry for a further 5-10 minutes.
Pour over the stock, then add the *bouquet garni*, thyme, pepper
and drained beans. Cover the pan and simmer gently for 2½
hours. Remove the *bouquet garni* before serving.
Serves 4-6

Foie d'agneau aux champignons
Lamb's liver with mushrooms

1 lb lamb's liver, cut in thin slices
flour
salt and pepper
2 tablespoons butter
1 tablespoon olive oil
6 oz mushrooms, finely chopped
1 tablespoon chopped parsley
1 tablespoon chopped chives
1 clove garlic, crushed
1 tablespoon lemon juice

Dust the liver with flour, seasoned with salt and pepper. Heat the
butter and oil in a frying pan. Add the liver to the pan and cook
on each side for 2 minutes. Add the remaining ingredients and
cook gently for a further 8 minutes or until the liver is tender.
Serves 4

Rognons d'agneau à la mode de Bourges
Lamb's kidneys with onions and mushrooms

2 tablespoons butter
3 shallots
4 to 8 small white onions
¼ lb button mushrooms
⅔ cup white wine
1 tablespoon tomato paste

pinch sugar
12 lamb's kidneys
salt and pepper

Melt the butter in a pan and fry the shallots, onions and mushrooms for about 5 minutes. Add the wine, tomato paste and sugar and cook for a further 10 minutes. Cut the kidneys in half and remove the cores. Add them to the pan and cook quickly for about 8 minutes. Taste and adjust the seasoning before serving.
Serves 4

Filet de porc normande
Pork tenderloin with mushrooms

1 ½ lb pork tenderloin
4 tablespoons flour
salt and pepper
1 ¼ cups white wine
½ lb button mushrooms
2 tablespoons butter
2 tablespoons Calvados (or use brandy)
⅔ cup heavy cream
2 tablespoons chopped parsley

Cut the pork into strips, about 1 ½ in long and ¼ in thick. Toss in the flour seasoned with salt and pepper. Pour the wine into a saucepan, add the mushrooms, cover and simmer gently for about 10 minutes. Melt the butter in a large frying pan, add the pork and fry quickly for about 8 minutes until all the pork is golden brown. Spoon over the Calvados or brandy, then ignite it. When the flames have died down, add the wine and mushrooms and simmer gently for a further 10 minutes or until the meat is tender. Add the cream and heat gently, without boiling. Spoon into a serving dish and sprinkle with the parsley.
Serves 4

Côtes de porc avesnoise
Pork chops with cheese

4 pork chops
salt and pepper
2 tablespoons butter
¾ cup grated Gruyère or Emmenthal cheese
2 teaspoons French mustard
3 tablespoons cream

Season the pork chops with salt and pepper, dot with butter and broil on both sides for 10 minutes or until golden brown and cooked through. Blend the grated cheese with the mustard and cream to make a thick paste. Divide this mixture between the pork chops and spread evenly all over the top of the chops to within about ½ in of the edge. Replace under the broiler for a couple of minutes or until the cheese is golden brown and bubbling. Serve at once.
Serves 4

Côtes de porc auvergnate
Pork chops with cabbage and cheese

1½ lb cabbage; a Savoy or similar type would be ideal
salt
2 tablespoons butter
1 large onion, finely chopped
1 clove garlic, crushed
4 pork chops
freshly milled black pepper
1¼ cups white wine
4 tablespoons heavy cream
½ cup grated Gruyère cheese

Finely shred the cabbage and cook in boiling salted water for 5 minutes. Drain and turn into a bowl. Melt 1 tablespoon of the butter in a frying pan, add the onion and garlic and fry gently for 10 minutes. Add the onion to the cabbage, mix lightly and turn half of it into the bottom of a buttered casserole. Heat the remainder of the butter in the frying pan, season the chops with salt and pepper and fry quickly on both sides until golden brown. Remove from the pan and place on the cabbage in the casserole and cover with the remaining cabbage. Pour the wine into the pan and keep over a moderate heat until the wine has reduced to about 4 tablespoons. Add the cream and heat gently, then pour over the cabbage. Sprinkle the grated cheese on top. Bake, uncovered, in a moderate oven (350°F) for about 45 minutes. *Serves 4*

Côtes de porc à la campagne
Marinated pork chops with herbs

You should start this recipe 2 days before you intend to eat it.

⅔ cup red wine
2 tablespoons vinegar
1 carrot, chopped
1 small onion, chopped
1 shallot, chopped
1 clove garlic, crushed
1 bay leaf
a few parsley stalks
1 sprig thyme
3 black peppercorns
3 juniper berries
1 teaspoon salt
4 thick pork chops, preferably from the loin
2 tablespoons butter
⅔ cup stock
1 level tablespoon redcurrant jelly

Put the wine, vinegar, carrot, onion, shallot, garlic, bay leaf,

parsley stalks, thyme, peppercorns, juniper berries and salt into a saucepan. Bring slowly to the boil and simmer for 2-3 minutes, then leave to cool. Put the chops into a shallow dish, pour over the cooled marinade and leave in a cold place for about 2 days, turning several times. Heat the butter in a frying pan and fry the chops for about 5 minutes on each side until golden brown. Pour over the strained marinade and the stock and cook gently for about 20 minutes, uncovered, or until the pork is tender. Remove the meat from the pan, place on a heated serving dish and keep warm. Add the jelly to the pan and cook for about 2-3 minutes. Pour over the chops and serve.
Serves 4

Côtes de porc provençale
Pork chops with tomatoes, mushrooms and garlic

4 large pork chops
salt and pepper
1 large clove garlic
4 tablespoons olive oil
¼ lb *cèpes* or button mushrooms
4 large tomatoes, skinned and coarsely chopped

Season the chops with salt and pepper. Chop the garlic very finely and press it into both sides of the chops. Heat the oil in a large frying pan and fry the pork chops for 10 minutes on each side. Remove them from the pan, place on a heated serving dish and keep warm. Add the *cèpes* or mushrooms to the pan and cook for 5 minutes, then add the tomatoes and seasoning and cook for a further 5 minutes. Spoon this mixture over the pork chops and serve.
Serves 4

Cassoulet
Haricot bean casserole

Cassoulet is an age-old peasant dish from the Languedoc. It is very filling, and was generally made in the winter months when fresh vegetables and meat were unobtainable and the people lived on vegetables they had dried during the summer and the salt pork, sausages and preserved goose they had cured during the autumn.

2⅔ cups haricot (dried white) beans
1 lb salt port
5½ cups stock
1 lb stewing lamb
¼ lb lean bacon, in one piece
2 tablespoons lard or dripping
1 large onion, chopped
2 cloves garlic, crushed
4 tablespoons tomato paste
1 bay leaf
1 sprig thyme
2 tablespoons chopped parsley
½ lb garlic sausage
⅔ cup fresh white or brown breadcrumbs

Soak the beans and pork overnight in cold water. Drain well. Turn the beans into a saucepan with the stock, cover and simmer for 1½ hours or until the beans are just tender. Cut the pork, lamb and bacon into 1-in cubes, discarding any skin and bone. Melt the lard or dripping in a heatproof dish and fry the onion, garlic, pork, lamb and bacon for about 10 minutes. Add the beans, together with the stock, tomato paste, herbs and garlic sausage. Mix well. Cover and cook in a very moderate oven (325°F) for 3 hours. Thirty minutes before the end of cooking, sprinkle the breadcrumbs over the top of the *cassoulet* and leave uncovered for the remainder of the cooking time.
Serves 6

Petit salé aux lentilles
Salt pork with lentils

This is a recipe from the Auvergne. As well as the salt pork with which the lentils are cooked, grilled sausages are often served with the dish.

1½-lb piece salt pork
1 cup lentils (see page 21)
1 onion, chopped
1 clove garlic, crushed
1 *bouquet garni*
salt

Cut the pork into 2-in cubes and discard any bones. Put into a bowl and cover with cold water. Leave for about 2 hours, then drain. Put the lentils, onion, garlic and *bouquet garni* into a saucepan. Add 3¾ cups of cold water and bring to the boil. Add the pork, cover and simmer gently for about 1¼ hours or until the lentils and pork are tender. About 20 minutes before the end of cooking, check how much water is left in the pan; if there is still quite a lot, leave the pan uncovered for the remainder of the cooking time. By the time the lentils and pork are tender, all the liquid should be absorbed. Remove *bouquet garni*. Taste the lentils and add salt, if necessary, before turning into a serving dish.
Serves 4

Chou rouge aux saucisses landais
Red cabbage with sausages

1 small to medium-sized red cabbage, shredded
1 lb cooking apples, peeled, cored and diced
1 lb onions, sliced
2 red or green peppers, cored, seeded and chopped
peeled zest ¼ orange, finely shredded
2 teaspoons salt

freshly milled black pepper
¼ teaspoon grated nutmeg
2 tablespoons sugar
4 cloves
1 clove garlic, crushed
⅔ cup red wine
⅔ cup wine vinegar
about 8-12 smoked sausages

In a large casserole put a layer of cabbage, then a layer of onions, apples and peppers. Sprinkle with a little of the salt, pepper, nutmeg, sugar, a clove, a little orange zest and a little of the garlic and repeat these layers until all these ingredients are used up. Pour in the wine and wine vinegar. Cover the dish tightly and cook in a very slow oven (300°F) for 3½ hours. Take the casserole out of the oven, bury the sausages deep into the dish and cook for a further 30 minutes.
Serves 4-6

Chou farci à la provençale
Stuffed cabbage Provençale

1 large crisp cabbage, ideally a Savoy
salt
1 tablespoon butter
¼ lb fat bacon, diced
½ cup cooked rice
2 large onions, chopped
¾ lb sausagemeat
½ lb tomatoes, skinned and shopped
½ lb spinach, finely chopped
1 stalk celery, finely chopped
2 cloves garlic, crushed

2 tablespoons chopped parsley
1 teaspoon finely chopped thyme
pepper
1 ¼ cups well-flavoured stock
2 carrots, chopped
2 leeks, chopped

Leave the cabbage whole, but remove about 5 of the large outside leaves. Cook both the cabbage and the leaves in a large pan of boiling, salted water for 4 minutes. Drain and rinse in cold water. Melt the butter in a pan and fry the bacon and one of the onions for about 8 minutes or until golden brown. Put into a bowl with the sausagemeat, tomatoes, spinach, celery, garlic, herbs and plenty of seasoning. Very carefully open out the cabbage, leaf by leaf and, starting in the centre, spread each leaf with a spoonful of the stuffing. Wrap the large leaves round the cabbage and tie it securely with string. Pour the stock into a large casserole, add the remaining onion, and the carrots and leeks. Place the cabbage in the middle, cover tightly with a lid and cook in a very moderate oven (325°F) for 3 hours.

Before serving, carefully take the string off the cabbage and arrange it on a serving dish with the drained vegetables from the pan; serve the stock separately.
Serves 6

Rognons de porc au vin rouge
Pig's kidneys in red wine

4 medium-sized pig's kidneys
2 tablespoons butter
4 strips lean bacon, finely chopped
½ lb mushrooms, roughly chopped
¾ cup red wine
1 *bouquet garni*
salt and pepper
2 tablespoons chopped parsley

Soak the kidneys in cold water for 3-4 hours, drain and dry well; this helps to remove some of the rather strong flavour. Slice the kidneys diagonally into ½-in pieces, discarding the core. Heat the butter in a pan, add the bacon and cook gently for a few minutes, then add the kidneys and mushrooms and cook for 2 minutes. Pour over the wine and let it reduce slightly, then add the *bouquet garni* and seasoning. Cover the pan and simmer gently for 15 minutes. Remove the *bouquet garni* and serve the kidneys sprinkled with the parsley.
Serves 4

Poultry and game

Deep-freezing and battery hen-houses have caused a mild revolution in eating habits. Some time ago chicken was a luxury dish to be eaten on Sundays about once a month if you were lucky. Now it has become an everyday dish and it has lost most of its flavour. Not even the most enthusiastic owner of a chicken deep-freezing plant would deny that the flavour of a chicken which has scratched around in the farmyard, has been killed and left to hang for a few days before being cleaned and cooked is far superior to anything he can produce. However, most of us now have to rely on these or on the fresh chickens from the butcher which are only marginally better, so we must make the best of them.

Firstly if you are using a frozen bird, it should be allowed to defrost slowly in the refrigerator for about 24 hours if possible. You should then wipe it dry with a cloth inside and out. I have found that the recipe for *poulet rôti à la française*, and *poulet au citron* really do make a frozen bird taste much nicer than plain roasting.

Poulet rôti à la francaise
French roast chicken

1 4-lb roasting chicken
6 tablespoons butter
salt and freshly milled black pepper
1 teaspoon chopped fresh tarragon

Wipe the chicken, inside and out, with a clean, dry cloth. Lightly cream the butter and add the seasoning and tarragon. Put about two-thirds of the butter inside the chicken and spread the rest of it all over the skin of the bird. Roast in a moderately hot oven (400°F) for 45 minutes, then lower the heat to (350°F) for a further 45 minutes. Baste with the juices several times during cooking. When the chicken is cooked, place it in a heated serving dish and pour the butter and juices into a sauceboat.
Serves 6

Variation

Poulet au citron
Chicken with lemon

Prepare the chicken as for *poulet rôti à la française*, above, but inside the chicken place the peeled zest of a lemon and about 2 tablespoons butter. Spread a further 2 tablespoons butter all over the bird and season with salt and pepper. Pour over the juice of the lemon. Roast as above.

Poulet farci aux pruneaux
Stuffed roast chicken with prunes

1 lb prunes
1 4-lb roasting chicken
1 lb sausagemeat
2 tablespoons raisins
2 slices white bread
milk
salt and pepper
pinch nutmeg
2 tablespoons butter

Soak the prunes overnight in cold water, then drain. Finely chop the chicken liver and heart and put into a bowl with the sausage-

meat, raisins and a few of the prunes, finely chopped. Remove the crusts from the bread and soak in milk for 5 minutes, then wring dry in your hands. Add to the sausagemeat with the seasoning and nutmeg and mix well. Use this mixture to stuff the chicken. Rub the chicken all over with the butter then put into a large, buttered ovenproof casserole. Roast in a moderately hot oven (375°F) for about 2 hours. Halfway through cooking add the remainder of the drained prunes to the dish, round the chicken. Baste from time to time during cooking, and serve the chicken in the casserole in which it was cooked.
Serves 6

Poulet au riz à la campagne
Pot-roast stuffed chicken

1 roasting chicken, about 4-5 lb
½ cup rice
salt
¼ cup raisins
2 stalks celery, finely chopped
2 tablespoons butter
1 lb onions
1 lb small tomatoes
1 lb carrots
4 tablespoons water or white wine
pepper

Wipe the chicken all over with a damp cloth. Cook the rice in boiling salted water until just tender. Drain well. Stir in the raisins, celery and butter. Use this mixture to stuff the chicken. Peel the onions and tomatoes. Peel or scrape the carrots; if they are small, leave them whole, if they are large, cut into quarters lengthways. Put the vegetables with the water or wine into the bottom of a casserole and season with salt and pepper. Place the chicken on top and season. Cover the casserole and cook in a moderate oven (350°F) for 2½ hours.
Serves 6

Coq au vin

This, one of the most famous chicken dishes in the world, comes from the Bourgogne. It should be made with a good Burgundy wine, but you can use another red wine, provided it is a full-bodied one.

1 chicken, about 3-4 lb
⅔ cup water
2 tablespoons butter
6 oz salt pork, cubed
1 lb small white onions, peeled
2 stalks celery, finely chopped
1 clove garlic, crushed
4 tablespoons flour
2 cups red Burgundy wine
1 bay leaf
1 sprig thyme
salt and pepper
½ lb button mushrooms
To garnish:
small triangles of fried bread

Simmer the chicken giblets in the water for about 30 minutes. Cut the chicken into 6 pieces. Melt the butter in a large heavy pan with a cover and fry the pork until golden brown. Remove from the pan and put on one side. Add the chicken to the pan and fry until golden brown on all sides, then put on one side with the pork. Add the onions, celery and garlic to the pan, and cook for a further 5 minutes. stirring frequently. Stir in the flour and simmer gently for about 5 minutes, then gradually add the wine and the strained stock from cooking the giblets. Bring to the boil, stirring all the time and add the pork and chicken and all the remaining ingredients, except the mushrooms. Cover and simmer gently for 1 hour. Add the mushrooms to the pan halfway through the cooking time. Before serving, skim off any excess fat from the sauce and remove the thyme and bay leaf. Turn into a serving dish and garnish with the triangles of fried bread.
Serves 6

Poulet niçoise
Chicken with tomatoes and olives

1 4 lb chicken
2 tablespoons flour
salt and pepper
3 tablespoons olive oil
½ lb small white onions
2 cloves garlic, crushed
1 lb tomatoes, skinned
about ¾ cup olives, pitted
1 *bouquet garni*
pinch saffron
1 ¼ cups white wine
juice 1 lemon

Cut the chicken in serving pieces, then sprinkle with the flour, seasoned with salt and pepper. Heat the olive oil in a wide, shallow pan and fry the chicken for about 10 minutes, or until golden brown all over. Lower the heat, add the onions and fry these for a further 5 minutes. Add the garlic, tomatoes, olives, *bouquet garni*, saffron and wine to the pan and bring to the boil. Lower the heat, cover, and simmer gently for 45 minutes or until the chicken is tender. Remove the pan from the heat, take out the *bouquet garni*, then stir in the lemon juice. Turn into a serving dish and serve.
Serves 6

Poulet sauté à la crème
Fried chicken with cream sauce

1 frying chicken
salt and pepper
2 tablespoons butter
1 tablespoon olive oil
1 *bouquet garni*
⅔ cup heavy cream
2 tablespoons chopped parsley

Quarter the chicken and season lightly with salt and pepper. Heat the butter and oil in a large, shallow pan and cook the chicken fairly quickly, turning the pieces until they are golden brown. Add the *bouquet garni*, lower the heat and cook for a further 20 minutes or until the meat is quite tender. Remove the chicken from the pan, place on a heated serving dish and keep warm. Pour the cream into the pan and heat gently for about 5 minutes. Remove the *bouquet garni*, pour the sauce over the chicken and sprinkle with chopped parsley.
Serves 4

Poulet Vallée d'Auge
Chicken with cider and apples

The Vallée d'Auge is one of the chief cider-growing districts of Normandy and it is also said to produce the best Calvados.

1 3-4 lb chicken, quartered or use breasts or thighs
salt and freshly milled black pepper
4 tablespoons butter
4 eating apples
¼ lb button mushrooms, finely chopped
1 ¼ cups dry cider
2 tablespoons Calvados
⅔ cup heavy cream

Season the chicken with salt and pepper. Melt half the butter in a saucepan and gently fry the chicken on all sides until golden brown. Peel, core and finely chop two of the apples, add to the chicken, cover and cook gently for 10 minutes. Put the mushrooms and cider into a separate pan and simmer for 10 minutes. Pour the Calvados over the chicken and set alight, then strain over the cider, reserving the mushrooms. Cover the pan and simmer the chicken very gently for about 30 minutes or until it is tender.

Peel and core the last 2 apples, and cut into rings. Heat the remaining butter in a frying pan and fry the apple rings for about 5 minutes, turning several times until golden brown.

Remove the chicken from the pan and place on a heated serving dish. Boil the cooking liquid rapidly until it is reduced to ⅔ cup. Stir in the cream and heat gently without boiling, for a few minutes. Stir in the mushrooms, cook for a further minute, then pour over the chicken. Garnish the dish with the fried apple rings.

Serves 4

Poulet à l'estragon
Tarragon chicken

1 4-lb roasting chicken
5 cups water
1 carrot, chopped
1 onion, chopped
2 stalks celery, chopped
few parsley stalks
salt and pepper
1 bunch tarragon
2 tablespoons butter
4 tablespoons flour
⅔ cup light cream
1 egg yolk

Put the chicken giblets into a saucepan with the water, carrot, onion, celery, parsley stalks and seasoning. Bring to the boil, remove any scum, cover and simmer gently for 1 hour. Add the chicken to the pan, cover and simmer gently for a further 1½ hours. Remove the chicken from the pan, place on a heated serving dish and keep warm. Add the tarragon to the stock in the pan and boil rapidly until it is reduced to about 2 cups. While the stock is reducing, melt the butter in a pan, add the flour and cook for a minute. Gradually strain in the reduced stock, then bring to the boil, stirring all the time. Blend the egg yolk with the cream

and stir into the sauce. Reheat gently without boiling, taste and adjust the seasoning and serve this sauce separately with the chicken.
Serves 6

Canard en gelée
Duck in jelly

2 tablespoons butter
1 tablespoon olive oil
1 4-lb duck
½ lb pork butt, cut in one piece
1 lb turnips, peeled and diced
½ lb small white onions, peeled
½ lb button mushrooms
⅔ cup white wine
2½ cups *fonds blanc* (see page 26)
1 *bouquet garni*
salt and pepper

Heat the butter and oil in a large pan, then quickly fry the duck on all sides until it is golden brown. Remove the duck from the pan. Cut the pork into 1-in cubes. Add the bacon, turnips, onions and mushrooms to the pan and cook for 10 minutes. Add the wine and stock, bring to the boil, then replace the duck in the pan with the *bouquet garni*, seasoning and duck giblets. Cover the pan and simmer gently for 2 hours or until the duck is tender. Remove the duck from the pan and place in a large terrine or ovenproof casserole. Surround with the pork, turnips, mushrooms and onions. Boil the stock (*fonds blanc*) rapidly until it is reduced to 2 cups. Allow it to cool slightly, then skim off the fat. Using a very fine-meshed sieve, strain the stock over the duck and refrigerate for about 8 hours or overnight. Serve the duck in the casserole.
Serves 4-6

Confit d'oie
Preserved goose

Preserved goose, a specialty of the south-western regions, is traditionally made by the farmers' wives in the autumn when the geese are killed off. This recipe is really only suitable for country dwellers who either rear their own geese or can buy them from a local farm, and who also have a dry, airy larder. If your home is kept very warm, you could keep the goose in a garage or garden shed, but it must be dry and cool. If properly stored the goose should keep for several months, but it is important to re-cover the jar or container with fat every time you remove a piece. The goose is generally used to supplement hearty winter fare, such as *cassoulet* (see page 164) and *garbure* (see page 30).

1 goose
¼ cup sea salt
pork fat or beef drippings (see method)

Cut the goose into pieces at the joints and remove all the fat from the inside. Rub the meat all over with the salt, place in an earthenware dish and leave for 5-6 days if it is a freshly killed farm goose, or 2-3 days if it is a shop goose. Melt the goose fat down; you should have enough to completely cover the goose when it is cooking, so if there is insufficient you will have to add a little pure pork fat or beef drippings.

At the end of the salting time, wash the goose and place in a deep casserole. Cover with the fat and cook in a moderate oven (350°F) for 2-3 hours or until the goose is quite tender. Pack the goose into a jar or other suitable container, allow the fat to cool a little then strain over the goose so that it is completely covered. Cover the jar with paper or foil and then use as required.

Oie à la poitevine
Goose with garlic and onions

1 goose, about 6-7 lb
2 tablespoons dripping
1 lb onions, sliced
8 cloves garlic
1 lb tomatoes
salt and pepper
2 tablespoons chopped parsley
1¼ cups white wine
1½ lb small white onions
1 tablespoon oil
1 tablespoon granulated sugar
4 tablespoons port wine

Wipe the goose all over and dry it. Heat the dripping in a roasting pan on top of the stove and quickly brown the goose all over. Remove it from the pan, add the onions, garlic, tomatoes, seasoning and parsley, and cook gently for 5 minutes. Replace the goose in the pan and add the white wine. Cover with foil and cook in a slow oven (325°F) for 4 hours, basting from time to time.

Peel the small white onions, heat the oil in a pan and gently fry the onions for about 15 minutes or until golden brown all over. Add the sugar and port and leave until syrupy. Remove the goose from the pan, place on a heated serving dish and keep warm. Carefully skim off all the fat from the vegetables and juices in the tin, then sieve into the glazed onions. Serve this sauce separately with the goose.

Serves 8

Dindonneau farci aux marrons
Turkey with chestnut stuffing

1 lb chestnuts
⅔ cup stock
1 bay leaf
1 sprig thyme
1 strip bacon, chopped
1 stalk celery, chopped
1 lb good sausagemeat
salt and pepper
¼ teaspoon grated nutmeg
2 tablespoons brandy
2 tablespoons chopped parsley
1 egg, lightly beaten
grated rind ½ lemon
1 10-lb turkey
4 tablespoons butter

Make a small slit in the top of each chestnut. Put the chestnuts into boiling water for 5 minutes, then peel off the shell. Keep the chestnuts in the water while you are peeling them and if you find halfway through that they are getting rather difficult to peel, replace the saucepan over the heat and bring back to the boil. Put the chestnuts into a saucepan with the stock, bay leaf, thyme, bacon and celery. Cover and simmer gently for 20 minutes or until the chestnuts are tender. Remove the herbs, bacon and celery and either put the chestnuts and stock into a blender and blend for a minute or sieve the chestnuts and blend with the stock. Put into a bowl and add the sausagemeat, seasoning, nutmeg, brandy, parsley, beaten egg and lemon rind. Mix well. Use this mixture to stuff the cavity of the bird. Spread the bird all over with butter and season with salt and pepper. Roast in a moderate oven (350°F) for 4 hours. Baste from time to time during cooking and if it is becoming too brown, cover with a piece of foil.
Serves up to 15

Lapin à la moutarde
Mustard rabbit

This method of preparing rabbit can transform a rather dull rabbit into something very special and in the hunting areas of France is often the *pièce de résistance* in the local restaurants.

1 large rabbit, about 3 lb
1¼ cups white wine
1 onion, chopped
2 carrots, chopped
few parsley stalks
1 sprig thyme
2 cloves
salt and pepper
1 pig's foot
1 tablespoon French mustard
¼ lb pork fat

Lay the rabbit in a long shallow dish and add the wine, onion, carrots, parsley, thyme, cloves and seasoning. Leave to marinate for 24 hours, turning from time to time.

Split the pig's foot in half and put into a saucepan of cold water. Bring to the boil and leave for 5 minutes, then drain. Cut the pork fat into thin slices. Remove the rabbit from the marinade, strain and reserve the liquid from the marinade. Dry the rabbit well, spread all over, inside and out, with the mustard, and lay the pig's foot inside. Cover the outside of the rabbit with pork fat and tie into place with string. Place it in a roasting pan and roast in a moderate oven (350°F) for 1¼ hours. Remove from the oven, remove the string, the fat and pig's foot. Arrange on a serving dish and keep warm. Add the strained marinade to the meat juices in the roasting pan and boil for about 5 minutes on top of the stove. Pour into a sauceboat and serve with the rabbit.
Serves 4

Lapin à la campagne
Rabbit stew

2 small rabbits
salt and pepper
4 strips lean bacon, roughly chopped
1 lb small white onions, peeled
1 tablespoon olive oil
3 tablespoons flour
⅔ cup water
⅔ cup red wine
¼ lb mushrooms
1 clove garlic, crushed
1 bay leaf

Cut the rabbits into serving pieces and season with salt and pepper. Put the bacon into a pan and cook over a gentle heat for 5 minutes or until the fat runs, then increase the heat slightly and add the onions. Fry lightly until golden brown, then remove the onions from the pan and add the oil and rabbit. Fry these for 5 minutes, or until they are brown, and remove from the pan with the bacon. Stir in the flour and cook over low heat for about 10 minutes until the flour is a rich brown colour, but do not allow it to burn. Gradually add the water and wine and bring to the boil, stirring all the time. Return the rabbit, bacon and onions to the pan with the remaining ingredients. Cover and simmer for about 1 hour or until the rabbit is quite tender.
Serves 6

Lapin au cidre
Cider rabbit

½ lb smoked pork butt
2½-lb rabbit cut into serving pieces
4 tablespoons flour
salt and pepper

4 shallots, finely chopped
2 cups dry cider
1 *bouquet garni*
2 tablespoons butter
½ lb button mushrooms

Cut the pork butt into ½-in pieces, put into a fireproof casserole and place over a low heat until the fat starts to run. Increase the heat and cook until brown, then remove from the pan and put on one side.

Toss the rabbit pieces in the flour seasoned with salt and pepper, add to the fat remaining in the dish with the shallots and fry until the rabbit is golden brown on all sides. Pour over the cider and bring to the boil. Add the *bouquet garni*, cover the casserole and put into a very moderate oven (325°F) for 1 hour.

Melt the butter in a frying pan and fry the mushrooms for about 10 minutes. Take the rabbit out of the oven, remove the *bouquet garni* and stir in the mushrooms and pork before serving.
Serves 4

Lièvre à la royale
Stuffed hare with red wine sauce

This is a good country way of cooking hare. Hare tends to be a rather dry meat, so before cooking it is a good idea to marinate it for about 24 hours in red wine with plenty of herbs and seasoning. This recipe seems like a lot of work, but the result is worth it.

1 hare, weighing about 5-6 lb
1½ lb pork belly
4 slices white bread
1 tablespoon chopped parsley
2 cloves garlic

2 shallots, finely chopped
salt and freshly milled black pepper
¼ teaspoon grated nutmeg
1 egg, lightly beaten
⅔ cup bacon trimmings or chopped bacon
⅔ cup stock
1 ¼ cups red wine
3 tablespoons brandy (optional)
2 onions, sliced
few parsley stalks
1 sprig thyme
1 small bay leaf
3 cloves
2 tablespoons butter
4 tablespoons flour

Ask the butcher to keep the blood of the hare for you or, if you have shot the hare yourself, leave it to hang with a bag over its head to catch all the blood. When the hare has been skinned and cleaned, wipe it well with a damp cloth.

Grind the pork and the liver from the hare and put into a bowl. Cut off the crusts from the bread, soak in cold water for 5 minutes, then squeeze it very dry with your hands. Add the pork with the chopped parsley, 1 of the cloves of garlic, finely crushed, the shallots, seasoning, nutmeg and egg. Mix together well and beat lightly with a wooden spoon. Use this mixture to stuff the paunch of the hare and sew up with coarse thread or string. Lay the hare in a large roasting pan, put the bacon trimming on top, add the stock, wine and brandy and sprinkle with the onions, parsley stalks, thyme, bay leaf, cloves, seasoning and remaining clove of garlic. Cover with a lid or foil and bake in a moderate oven (350°F) for 3 hours. Remove from the oven and place the hare on a heated serving dish. Skim off the fat, strain the juices into a clean saucepan and bring to the boil. Cream the butter with the flour and add this paste gradually, a teaspoon at a time to the boiling liquid, stirring well between each addition. Lower the

heat and stir in the blood of the hare. *Do not* allow the sauce to boil after the blood has been added or it will curdle. Serve this sauce separately with the hare.
Serves 6-8

Pintade en cocotte à la crème
Braised guinea fowl with cream

1 tablespoon olive oil
2 tablespoons butter
2 guinea fowl
3 heads celery
⅔ cup dry white wine
⅔ cup water
salt and pepper
⅔ cup heavy cream

Heat the butter and oil in a large pan and quickly fry the guinea fowl so that they are golden brown all over. Remove them from the pan. Scrub the celery, trim off the leaves and cut in half lengthways. Add the celery to the pan and fry quickly until golden brown. Pour in the wine and water and season with salt and pepper. Bring to the boil, replace the guinea fowl in the pan, cover and simmer gently for 1½ hours or until the guinea fowl are tender. Remove the birds from the pan and place on a heated serving dish with the celery arranged round. Keep hot. Boil the liquid remaining in the pan rapidly until it is reduced to 1 cup, then add the cream and mix well. Heat gently without boiling, taste and adjust the seasoning. Serve this sauce separately with the guinea fowl.
Serves 6

Faisan en casserole
Casseroled pheasant with port

If you're not sure how old a pheasant is, this is a good way of cooking it.

1 large pheasant
1 tablespoon olive oil
2 tablespoons butter
1 large onion, sliced
½ cup flour
2 cups stock
grated zest and juice of 1 orange
1 tablespoon redcurrant jelly
⅔ cup port wine
1 bay leaf
1 sprig parsley
salt and pepper

Cut the pheasant into quarters. Heat the oil and butter in a pan and quickly fry the pheasant on all sides until it is well browned. Remove from the pan and place in a casserole. Add the onion to the pan and cook until soft. Then add the flour and cook, stirring, for a few minutes until golden brown. Gradually add the stock, and bring to the boil, stirring all the time. Allow to thicken before adding the remaining ingredients. Pour over the pheasant, cover, and cook in a very moderate oven (325°F) for about 3 hours, or until tender.
Serves 4

Estouffade de pigeons
Pigeon casserole

8 strips lean bacon
4 wood pigeons
2 tablespoons drippings
¼ lb small white onions

½ lb button mushrooms
⅔ cup white or red wine
salt and pepper
1 *bouquet garni*

Tie two bacon strips round each pigeon. Melt the dripping in a frying pan and fry the pigeons on all sides until golden brown. Remove from the pan and place in a casserole. Add the onions and mushrooms to the pan and cook for a further 8 minutes or until the onions are golden. Add the wine, seasoning and *bouquet garni* to the pan and bring just to the boil. Spoon over the pigeons, cover the casserole and cook in a very moderate oven (325°) for about 2 hours or until the pigeons are tender. *Serves 4*

Perdrix au chou
Casseroled partridge with cabbage

1 large cabbage
salt
2 tablespoons drippings
2 medium-sized partridges
½ lb lean bacon, cut in one piece
2 large carrots, chopped
1 *bouquet garni*
2 cloves garlic, crushed
4 smoked sausages
pepper
1¼ cups stock

Roughly chop the cabbage and cook in boiling salted water for about 8 minutes, then drain. Melt the drippings in a pan, add the partridge and cook on all sides until golden brown; remove from the pan. Cut the bacon into 1-in cubes, then fry this in the drippings remaining in the pan for 5 minutes. Put half the

cabbage in the bottom of the casserole. Add the partridge, the bacon cubes, carrots, *bouquet garni*, garlic sausages and seasoning, then cover with the remainder of the cabbage. Pour the stock over, cover the casserole and cook in a very moderate oven (325°F) for about 3 hours. Remove the casserole from the oven and place the cabbage on a serving dish. Joint the partridge and arrange this on the dish with the bacon and sausages.
Serves 4

Vegetables

In a French meal it is common for the vegetables to form a complete course of their own instead of being served as part of the main dish. It is therefore not surprising that the French have developed some excellent, although very often simple, methods of cooking vegetables. Potatoes are served in a wide variety of ways, although one of the most popular is *pommes frites*. I have not given a recipe for these as they really are only deep-fried potatoes, but one point you might like to remember if you do want to make them is that the French generally cut the potatoes about half the thickness of the standard American "French fry," which tends to make them crisper and less greasy.

Even if you do not want to serve your vegetables as a separate course, it is still worth while taking time and trouble over them. I always feel that a very good way to judge a restaurant is the choice of vegetables, and the way in which they cook and serve them. It is now possible to buy zucchini, green beans, snow peas and other rather more unusual vegetables quite often during the year, so try being more adventurous with the vegetables you serve.

Asperges à la sauce hollandaise
Asparagus with hollandaise sauce

The Sologne, the famous hunting area of France, is also renowned for its asparagus and each year an 'Asparagus Festival' is held in the village of Tigy. The Vineuil Saint-Cloud variety which is said to be the 'Queen of Asparagus' is grown near the *château* of Chambord.

1½ lb asparagus
salt
sauce hollandaise (see page 53)

Trim off the white and brown jagged ends of the asparagus and cut all the stalks to about the same length. Scrape off the rough skin near the cut end with a sharp knife, then wash in cold water. Tie the asparagus into neat and manageable bundles. Choose a pan which is either wide enough to take the bunch of asparagus lying down, or deep enough to take it standing up. Put in sufficient water to almost cover the asparagus, add salt and bring to the boil. Add the asparagus, bring back to the boil, cover, lower the heat and simmer for about 15 minutes or until the asparagus is just tender. Lift the asparagus carefully out of the pan, drain and serve hot with *sauce hollandaise*.

Asperges au beurre

Cook the asparagus as above and serve with melted butter.

Asperges vinaigrette

Cook the asparagus as above, allow to cool and serve cold with *sauce vinaigrette* (see page 52).

Macaroni à la languedocienne
Macaroni with eggplant

2 small eggplants
salt
4 tablespoons olive oil
4 large tomatoes, skinned and chopped
2 cloves garlic
1 sprig thyme

¼ lb mushrooms, sliced
pepper
pinch sugar
½ lb macaroni
2 tablespoons butter
1 cup grated Gruyère cheese

Cut the eggplants into thin slices, put into a colander and sprinkle
with 2 teaspoons of salt. Leave for 30 minutes. Heat the oil in a
pan and gently fry the eggplants, tomatoes, garlic, thyme
and mushrooms for about 30 minutes. Season well with pepper
and salt, if necessary, and add the sugar. Cook the macaroni in a
large pan of boiling salted water until it is just tender — do not
overcook. Drain and rinse it in cold water, then return to the pan
with the butter and toss gently for about 3 minutes. Turn the
macaroni into a heated serving dish, spoon the eggplant mixture
over it and sprinkle with cheese.
Serves 4

Haricots bretonne
Haricot beans, Brittany-style

Haricots bretonne are a traditional garnish for the salt meadow
lamb from Brittany, but make a good accompaniment to many
other dishes, and if a recipe is described as being *à la bretonne*, it
almost always has this garnish.

1⅓ cups haricot (dried white) beans
2 onions
2 cloves
1 *bouquet garni*
1 clove garlic, crushed
1 strip lean bacon, chopped
salt and pepper
2 tablespoons butter
1 tablespoon tomato paste
1 tablespoon chopped parsley

Cover the beans with cold water and leave to soak overnight. Peel one of the onions and stick the cloves into it. Put the drained beans into a saucepan with fresh water to cover, the clove-stuck onion, the *bouquet garni*, garlic, bacon and seasoning. Cover and simmer gently for 1½ hours or until the beans are tender. Drain, reserving 1¼ cups of the liquid from cooking. Finely chop the remaining onion. Melt the butter in a pan and fry the onion gently for about 5 minutes, then add the tomato paste and reserved bean stock. Cover and simmer gently for 10 minutes. Add the drained beans and simmer for a further 10 minutes. Serve sprinkled with parsley.
Serves 4

Cèpes farcis
Stuffed mushrooms

8 large flat *cèpes* or mushrooms
2 tablespoons butter
1 slice bread
little milk
1 tablespoon chopped parsley
1 small onion, very finely chopped
1 clove garlic, crushed
salt and pepper
4 tablespoons white wine

Take out the mushroom stems and chop finely. Fry the mushroom caps in the butter for about 5 minutes, then remove from the pan. Remove the crusts from the bread and soak the bread in the milk for a few minutes, then wring almost dry. Put into a bowl with the chopped mushroom stalks, parsley, onion and garlic. Season well with salt and pepper. Lay the mushroom caps in a greased ovenproof dish and divide the stuffing mixture between them. Sprinkle over the wine, cover and bake in a moderate oven (350°F) for 20 minutes.
Serves 4

Cèpes à la crème
Mushrooms in cream

½ lb *cèpes* or button mushrooms
2 tablespoons butter
1 tablespoon olive oil
1 small onion, very finely chopped
salt and pepper
⅓ cup heavy cream
2 tablespoons chopped parsley

Wash the *cèpes* or mushrooms and dry well. Heat the butter and oil in a pan and gently cook the onion and mushrooms with seasoning for about 15 minutes. Stir in the cream, heat gently then turn into a heated serving dish. Sprinkle with chopped parsley before serving.
Serves 4

Carottes Vichy

This is one of the best known French vegetable dishes and, to follow the old recipes properly, the carrots should be cooked in Vichy water, but this is not essential. It is one of the most delicious ways of cooking carrots, but perhaps another reason for its popularity is that both carrots and Vichy water are said to be good for the liver, and the French are well-known for a pre-occupation with their livers!

1 lb carrots
4 tablespoons butter
1 teaspoon sugar
pinch of salt
1 ¼ cups water
freshly milled black pepper
1 tablespoon chopped parsley or chervil

Peel the carrots and slice them thinly. Put into a saucepan with

half of the butter, the sugar, salt and water. Bring to the boil and cook, uncovered, for about 25 minutes until almost all the liquid has evaporated. It is important to shake the pan fairly frequently during cooking, particularly towards the end, so that the carrots do not burn and stick. Add the remaining butter, pepper and parsley, mix well and serve.
Serves 3-4

Carottes à la nivernaise
Glazed carrots

This is a classic French garnish, and the carrots are generally mixed with little onions as well. For this garnish, the carrots are cut into small ovals, rather like an olive, but this is not essential.

1 lb carrots
salt
2 tablespoons good meat stock
pinch of sugar
2 tablespoons butter

Peel the carrots and either cut into pieces the size and shape of an olive, or slice. Cook in a little boiling salted water until tender, then drain. Return to the pan and add the meat stock, sugar and butter. Put, uncovered, over a medium heat, tossing fairly frequently for about 5 minutes or until the carrots are glazed.
Serves 4

Topinambours aux tomates
Jerusalem artichokes with tomatoes

2 lb Jerusalem artichokes
salt
2 tablespoons olive oil
2 large tomatoes, skinned and chopped

2 cloves garlic, crushed
1 small onion, finely chopped
½ teaspoon chopped thyme
pepper
2 tablespoons chopped parsley

Peel the artichokes and cut into ¼-in slices. Cook in boiling salted water for about 20 minutes, or until just tender. Drain well. While the artichokes are cooking, heat the oil in a pan and fry the tomatoes, garlic, onion and thyme together for about 10 minutes. Add the drained artichokes and mix well. Season with salt and pepper, then tip into a serving dish and sprinkle with the chopped parsley.
Serves 4-6

Pâte aux pommes de terre
Potato pie

The old-fashioned name for this dish was *truffat*, because potatoes were said to be the truffles of the poor! It sounds very heavy and solid, but in fact is excellent and goes very well with grilled bacon or ham.

pâte brisée made with 2 cups flour (see page 223)
2 oz pork fat
1 large onion, chopped
1 ½ lb potatoes
salt and pepper
2 tablespoons chopped parsley
milk
⅓ cup heavy cream

Roll out the pastry and cut into 2 circles about 11 in and 9 in in diameter. Carefully press the larger circle into the bottom of 9-in flan ring or pan, so that there is a narrow rim of pastry round the top.
    Cut the pork fat into very thin strips and put into a bowl with

the onion. Peel the potatoes and slice thinly, add to the onion and pork with the seasoning and parsley and mix well. Put the potato mixture into the pastry case. Brush the edges of the pastry with a little milk, then cover with the second pastry circle. Pinch the edges well to seal the pastry, then trim them. Make a hole about ½ in in diameter in the centre of the pastry. Bake in a moderate oven (350°F) for 1½ hours. Fifteen minutes before the end of cooking, remove the pie from the oven and carefully pour the cream in through the hole in the centre. If the pie is becoming a little too brown, cover with foil.
Serves 8

Galette de pommes de terre
Potato cake

2 lb potatoes
salt
4 tablespoons butter
freshly milled black pepper
1 tablespoon flour
2 eggs, beaten

Scrub the potatoes, but do not peel them. Cook in boiling salted water for about 30 minutes or until tender. Drain, and when cool enough to handle, peel and then mash the potatoes. Add the butter, pepper, flour and most of the beaten eggs, reserving about 2 tablespoons. Press into a well-buttered ovenproof casserole, and then brush the top with the remaining egg. Bake in a moderate oven (350-375°F) for about 20 minutes until golden brown.
Serves 4-6

Pommes Dauphine
Fried potato puffs

1 lb potatoes
salt
pepper
pâte à choux made with ½ cup + 2 tablespoons flour
(see page 225)
deep oil or fat for frying

Scrub the potatoes well, but do not peel them. Put into a sauce-pan of boiling salted water and cook until they are just tender. Drain the potatoes, peel them and then sieve or mash so that there are no lumps at all. Season the potato well with extra salt and pepper. Make up the *pâte à choux* and then beat in the potato purée. Heat the oil or fat until a small piece of the mixture dropped into it sizzles and turns golden brown. Drop teaspoon-fuls of the mixture into the hot fat a few at a time and cook until they are golden brown and puffed up. Remove with a draining spoon and dry on kitchen paper. Serve as soon as possible after cooking.
Serves 4-6

Pommes de terre lyonnaise
Sauteed potatoes with onions

1 ½ lb potatoes
salt
6 tablespoons butter
2 onions
freshly milled black pepper
2 tablespoons chopped parsley

Scrub the potatoes well, but do not peel them. Put into a sauce-pan of boiling salted water and cook until they are just tender, then drain. When cool enough to handle, peel and cut them into ¼-in slices. Heat 4 tablespoons of the butter in a large frying

pan and fry the potatoes until they are crisp and golden brown, turning them several times; this will take about 15 minutes. Peel and thinly slice the onions. Heat the remaining butter in a separate frying pan and fry the onions until they are also golden. Add the onions to the potatoes, stir them lightly, and season with salt and pepper. Turn into a serving dish and sprinkle with parsley.
Serves 4-6

Oignons au four
Oven-baked onions

This is an old country way of cooking onions from the days when people did not have ovens in their homes and used to take food along to the baker's to be cooked with the bread if there was room, or as the oven was cooling after baking.

4 large onions
salt and pepper
2 tablespoons butter

Place the unpeeled onions on a baking tray and bake in a moderately hot oven (400°F) for 1½ hours. Remove from the oven, and holding the cooked onion in an oven mitt, carefully remove the dry brown skin. Put into a serving dish, sprinkle with salt and pepper and dot with butter.
Serves 4

Petits pois à la française
Peas, French-style

This is an excellent way of cooking peas; it gives additional flavour to frozen peas, makes fresh young peas superb and is also good for cooking rather older peas if they are given slightly longer cooking than in the recipe.

1 ½ lb freshly shelled, or frozen, peas
1 lettuce heart, finely shredded
1 bunch green onions, chopped
½ teaspoon salt
pinch sugar
½ cup boiling water
4 tablespoons butter
2 teaspoons flour
freshly milled black pepper

Put the peas, lettuce, green onions, salt and sugar into a saucepan and add the boiling water. Cover and cook gently for about 20 minutes or until the peas are quite tender. Cream a little of the butter with the flour and add this mixture a spoonful at a time to the peas, stirring well between each addition. Cook gently for about 2 minutes. Stir in the remainder of the butter, taste and adjust the seasoning before serving.
Serves 4-6

Desserts

The French are not as "dessert-conscious" as the British or Americans, and meals frequently end with cheese and a variety of fresh fruit. In summer, especially in the south, this may often consist of fresh figs, apricots, and peaches, as well as the usual oranges, apples and pears. In this chapter you will find that several of the recipes would classify as *haute cuisine*, but nevertheless there are still some good country-type desserts, such as *clafouti aux cerises* (page 215), and *poires agenaises* (page 217).

Crème pâtissière
Confectioners' custard

2 eggs
¼ cup vanilla sugar
2 tablespoons flour
1¼ cups milk
2 tablespoons unsalted butter

If you don't have any vanilla sugar, add a few drops of vanilla extract to superfine sugar. Blend together the eggs, sugar and flour. Bring the milk to the boil and pour onto the egg mixture, stirring continuously. Bring the mixture back to the boil, stirring all the time. Remove from the heat and stir in the butter. Cover the saucepan with a circle of damp parchment paper and leave the custard until it is cold. Use as required.
Makes 1¼ cups

Crème Chantilly

This is sweetened whipped cream which has a whisked egg white folded into it, making it lighter and helping to make it go further.

½ cup + 2 tablespoons heavy cream
1 egg white
1 tablespoon superfine sugar

Lightly whip the cream and beat the egg white until it stands in soft peaks. Carefully fold the egg white and sugar into the whipped cream, then put into a serving bowl.
Serves 6

Coeurs à la crème
Cheese hearts

Traditionally this dessert is made in small, heart-shaped moulds, either of tin or china, but it can be made very satisfactorily in a small sieve or colander.

8 oz cottage cheese
1 ¼ cups heavy cream
2-3 tablespoons superfine sugar
fresh fruit for serving—strawberries, raspberries, peaches or blackcurrants

Sieve the cottage cheese into a bowl. Stir in the cream and sugar and mix well. Line either small moulds or a sieve or colander with muslin and press the cheese mixture into the moulds or sieve. Leave overnight in the refrigerator to drain. Unmould the cheeses, arrange on a serving dish and surround with fresh fruit. Serve with extra sugar and fresh cream.
Serves 6

Glace pralinée
Praline ice cream

¼ cup superfine sugar
2 tablespoons water
2 oz shelled, unblanched almonds
4 eggs, separated
⅔ cup sifted sugar (confectioner's)
1 ¼ cups heavy cream, lightly whipped

Put the superfine sugar and water into a small, heavy saucepan and place over a gentle heat until the sugar has dissolved. Add the almonds and cook rapidly, stirring frequently, until the mixture turns a deep golden brown. Turn out onto an oiled baking sheet and leave until set. To crush the praline, either put into a blender and blend for a minute or place between double sheets of parchment paper and crush with a rolling pin.

Whisk the egg yolks with half the icing sugar. Beat the egg whites until very stiff, and then gradually beat in the remaining confectioner's sugar a teaspoon at a time. Beat the egg yolks gradually into the meringue mixture, then add the praline. Carefully fold in the cream, turn into a plastic container and freeze. Serve the ice cream with crisp cookies, such as *cigarettes* (see page 243).
Serves 8

Crème au moka
Mocha cream

6 oz semi-sweet baking chocolate
3 tablespoons strong, sweetened black coffee
4 eggs, separated
½ cup + 2 tablespoons heavy cream, lightly whipped

Break the chocolate into small pieces, put into a large bowl with

the coffee and stand over a pan of hot, but not simmering, water until the chocolate has melted. Remove from the heat and beat in the egg yolks, one at a time. Beat the egg whites until they form soft peaks. Fold half the lightly whipped cream, then the egg whites, into the chocolate mixture. Turn into a serving dish and chill for at least 1 hour. Pipe or spoon the remaining cream round the edge of the dish before serving.
Serves 6

Gelée au porto
Port wine jelly

1 ¼ cups water
peeled zest and juice 1 lemon
1 1-in cinnamon stick
1 tablespoon redcurrant jelly
¾ cup port wine
sugar
1 tablespoon or 1 envelope unflavored gelatine

Put the water, lemon zest, cinnamon stick and jelly into a saucepan. Bring to the boil and simmer for 10 minutes. Add the port and lemon juice and sweeten to taste (the amount of sugar needed will depend on the kind of port used). Heat until just below boiling point. Meanwhile soften the gelatine in 3 tablespoons of cold water. Remove the port mixture from the heat and stir in the softened gelatine until it dissolves completely. Strain into a measure and make up to 2 ½ cups with cold water if necessary. Pour into a glass dish or mould and leave until set. If using a mould, turn out before serving. Serve with cream.
Serves 4

Crème au vin blanc
White wine cream

This dessert should not be completed more than about 1 hour before serving as the mixture tends to separate, but even if it does it still tastes just as good.

1 tablespoon flour
½ cup sugar
6 eggs, separated
2½ cups white wine

Mix the flour with the sugar and egg yolks, then add the wine. Put into a saucepan and bring to the boil, stirring all the time until the mixture thickens. Remove from the heat, cover with a circle of damp parchment paper and leave until quite cold. Beat the egg whites until they form stiff peaks then fold these into the custard mixture. Chill until ready to serve.
Serves 6-8

Crème renversée
Caramel cream

While this is the classic way of making *crème caramel*, I find that children much prefer it if you bake the custard without the caramel. When the custard is cool, you make the caramel as in the recipe below and spoon it over the top. It hardens and the children seem to take great delight in trying to crack it!

3 tablespoons granulated sugar
3 tablespoons water
4 eggs
¼ cup superfine sugar
few drops vanilla extract
2½ cups milk

Put the granulated sugar and water into a pan and heat gently until the sugar has dissolved, then boil rapidly until the syrup turns a pale golden colour. Quickly pour this into the bottom of a pan or ovenproof dish. (Alternatively, the mixture may be divided between four individual ovenproof dishes.) Blend the eggs with the superfine sugar and vanilla extract. Heat the milk until it is just warm, then pour onto the egg mixture, stirring well.

Lightly butter the pan or ovenproof dish above the caramel, then strain the custard over the caramel. Cover the pan or dish and stand it in a roasting pan containing 1 in of cold water. Bake in a very slow oven (300°F) for 1½-2 hours or until a knife inserted in the centre comes out clean. Remove the dish from the oven, allow to cool, then chill for several hours. Turn out the pan just before serving.
Serves 4

Îles flottantes
Floating islands

2½ cups milk
2 large eggs, separated
½ cup superfine sugar
1 vanilla bean or a few drops vanilla extract
2 tablespoons brandy or rum (optional)
3 tablespoons water
3 tablespoons granulated sugar

Pour the milk into a shallow pan or deep frying pan and heat to simmering point. Beat the egg whites stiffly and then gradually beat in half the superfine sugar. Drop spoonfuls of the meringue mixture on top of the hot milk. Poach for 2 minutes, then turn with a perforated spoon or spatula and poach for the same time on the second side. Lift the meringues from the milk and drain on paper towel.

Beat the egg yolks in a basin with the remaining superfine sugar and pour over the milk. Add the vanilla bean or extract and turn into the top of a double boiler or a bowl over a pan of hot

water. Cook over low heat, stirring, until the custard coats the back of a wooden spoon. Remove the vanilla bean and add the brandy or rum, if using. Pour into a shallow dish and allow to cool. Top with the meringue balls and chill for about 2 hours. Put the water and sugar into a saucepan over a low heat until the sugar dissolves. Boil rapidly until the mixture turns golden brown, then spoon over the meringues.
Serves 4

Bavarois au chocolat
Chocolate cream mould

1 tablespoon or 1 envelope unflavored gelatine
4 tablespoons water
4 egg yolks
¼ cup superfine sugar
2½ cups milk
1 vanilla bean or 1 teaspoon vanilla extract
8 oz semi-sweet baking chocolate
1¼ cups heavy cream
chocolate curls to decorate

Sprinkle the gelatine over the water in a bowl and put on one side. Beat the egg yolks and sugar together for about 5 minutes. Heat the milk in a saucepan, then stir into the egg yolks and sugar. Blend well and strain into the top of a double boiler or a bowl over a pan of hot water. Add the vanilla bean or vanilla extract. Cook gently, stirring all the time until the mixture thickens and coats the back of a wooden spoon. Break the chocolate into small pieces, add to the pan and stir until melted. Remove the top of the double boiler or the bowl from the heat and stir in the gelatine. Stir until the gelatine has dissolved, then remove the vanilla bean, if used. Put in a cold place until the mixture begins to thicken. Lightly whip the cream and fold into the chocolate mixture when it is thick, but not set. Turn into a very lightly oiled mould or

pan and leave in a cold place. Turn out onto a serving plate and decorate with the chocolate curls.
Serves 8

Bavarois au rhum

Make as for the *bavarois au chocolat* (above), but fold in 3 table-spoons rum with the heavy cream.

Saint-Émilion au chocolat
Macaroons with chocolate

12 macaroons
4 tablespoons rum
½ cup butter
½ cup superfine sugar
⅓ cup milk
1 egg
8 oz unsweetened baking chocolate

Put the macaroons on a flat dish and sprinkle lightly with the rum. Cream the butter and sugar together until light and fluffy. Put the milk into a saucepan and bring to the boil. Remove from the heat, leave for about 10 minutes to cool, then beat in the egg. Put the chocolate into a basin over a pan of hot, not boiling, water and leave until melted. While the chocolate is still over the heat, beat in the milk then the butter and sugar. Beat the sauce well until it is very smooth. Put 4 of the macaroons into the bottom of a serving dish. Pour over half the chocolate sauce, top with 4 more macaroons, the remaining chocolate sauce and finally the macaroons. Place the dish in the refrigerator and chill for at least 12 hours.
Serves 6-8

Gâteau de marrons
Chestnut mould

1 lb chestnuts
⅓ cup milk
½ cup sugar
grated zest and juice 1 small orange
3 tablespoons water
1 tablespoon rum or brandy
2 egg whites

Make a slit in each chestnut with a sharp knife and cook in boiling water for 5 minutes, then peel off the shells. The chestnuts must be left in hot water until they are to be peeled and if, halfway through peeling them, you find the brown skins are becoming difficult to peel off, the pan should be replaced on the heat. Put the shelled nuts into a pan with the milk, half the sugar and the orange zest and simmer gently for 20 minutes or until they are tender. Put the remainder of the sugar and the water into a small saucepan, heat gently until the sugar has dissolved, then boil rapidly until the syrup turns a pale golden brown. Remove from the heat and quickly pour into the bottom of a lightly greased 6-in cake pan. Leave to cool.

Either put the chestnuts with half the milk used for cooking them into a blender and blend for a minute, or put them through a sieve and then blend with half the milk. Add the orange juice and rum or brandy. Beat the egg whites until they form soft peaks, then fold into the chestnut purée. Spoon this mixture into the cake pan and stand the pan in a roasting pan containing 1 in cold water. Bake in a very moderate oven (325°F) for 35-40 minutes. Leave to cool, then chill. Turn out of the pan just before serving.

Serves 4

Soufflé au chocolat et aux marrons
Chocolate chestnut souffle

1 lb chestnuts ⎤
⅓ cup milk ⎬ or use a 14-oz can sweetened
¼ cup sugar ⎦ chestnut purée
6 oz unsweetened baking chocolate
4 eggs, separated
⅓ cup cream

Peel the chestnuts (see *gâteau de marrons*, above) and put into a pan with the milk and sugar. Simmer gently for 20 minutes or until they are tender. Either put the chestnuts with the milk into a blender and blend for a minute, or put the chestnuts through a sieve and blend with the milk. Replace the chestnut purée in the saucepan and put over low heat. When almost boiling, remove from the heat and stir in the chocolate, broken up into small pieces. Stir until the chocolate has melted, then beat in the egg yolks one at a time. Lightly whip the ceam, and beat the egg whites until they stand in stiff peaks. Fold first the cream, then the egg whites, into the chocolate mixture. Turn into a serving dish and chill until required.
Serves 6-8

Vacherin aux marrons
Meringue cake with chestnuts

4 egg whites
1 cup superfine sugar
1 lb chestnuts ⎤
⅓ cup milk ⎬ or use a 14-oz can sweetened
¼ cup sugar ⎦ chestnut purée
2 tablespoons brandy or rum
juice ½ orange
⅔ cup cream, lightly whipped
marrons glacés to decorate (optional)

Draw an 8-in circle on a piece of parchment paper. Place on a greased baking sheet and brush lightly with oil. Beat the egg whites until they form stiff peaks. Beat in half the sugar a teaspoonful at a time, beating well between each addition. Fold in the remainder of the sugar. Spread just under half the meringue over the paper to fill the circle and smooth with a knife. Using either a piping bag and ½-in rose nozzle or two teaspoons, pile mounds of meringue all the way round the outside edge of the meringue circle. Bake the meringue in a very slow oven (225°F) for about 6 hours. Take out of the oven, leave to cool, then peel off the paper.

Peel the chestnuts (see *gâteau de marrons*, page 209), put into a small saucepan with the milk and sugar and simmer gently for about 20 minutes or until they are tender. Either put the chestnuts and milk used for cooking into a blender and blend for a minute, or put them through a sieve and blend with the milk. Allow to cool. When quite cold, stir in the brandy or rum and orange juice and fold in the lightly whipped cream. Spoon into the centre of the meringue case and decorate with *marrons glacés* if wished.
Serves 8

Crème Saint-Valentin
Cheese and coffee cream

8 oz light cream cheese
3 eggs, separated
¼ cup sugar
2 teaspoons instant coffee

Beat together the cheese, egg yolks, sugar and coffee. Leave to stand for 10 minutes for the coffee to dissolve, then beat again. Beat the egg whites until they stand in soft peaks, then fold into the cheese mixture. Turn into small, individual dishes and chill.
Serves 6

Pain perdu
Bread dipped in egg and fried with cinnamon and sugar

This is a sweet French version of American "French toast."

few drops vanilla extract
1¼ cups milk
8 slices stale French bread, abut ½ in thick
oil for frying
2 eggs, beaten
¼ cup superfine or powdered sugar
¼ teaspoon ground cinnamon

Add the vanilla extract to the milk and mix well. Soak the bread in the milk for about 5 minutes. Heat the oil in a frying pan. Quickly dip the bread in the beaten eggs, using two spoons to turn it, then fry in the hot oil until the bread is crisp and golden brown. Turn once during cooking. Put the fried bread onto a serving plate and sprinkle generously with the sugar mixed with the cinnamon.
Serves 4

Crêpes
Pancakes

This is a basic pancake mixture which can be used for both savoury and sweet stuffed pancakes. You will find fillings for sweet pancakes given on pages 214-15. If you wish to serve stuffed pancakes it is best to make all the pancakes first, then fill them and place in an ovenproof dish. Cover lightly with foil and bake in a moderately hot oven (375°F) for about 15 minutes.

4 tablespoons butter
1 cup flour

¼ teaspoon salt
2 eggs
1 cup milk
lard or oil for frying

Melt the butter and leave to cool. Sift the flour and salt into a bowl. Add the eggs, then gradually beat in the milk and butter to make a smooth batter. Lightly grease a frying pan with lard or oil and put over the heat until hot. Quickly pour in enough batter (about 2-3 tablespoons) to cover the bottom of the pan thinly, tilting the pan to achieve an even coverage. Cook until the underside of the pancake is golden brown, then turn or toss and cook on the other side until golden. When cooked pile the pancakes onto a plate, separating each one with a sheet of parchment or wax paper.
Makes about 8 pancakes

Omelette soufflé
Soufflé omelette

2 eggs, separated
1 tablespoon superfine sugar
1 tablespoon butter
filling (see page 214)

Beat the egg yolks with the sugar until light and creamy. Beat the egg whites until they are stiff and stand in soft peaks, then fold into the egg yolk mixture. Heat the butter in an all-metal omelette pan about 6-7 in in diameter until it is bubbling, add the mixture and spead it evenly over the pan. Allow to cook for about 4 minutes, then place the pan under a moderate broiler for about 6 minutes until the omelette is golden brown. Fill the omelette while it is in the pan, fold in half and slide out of the pan onto a serving plate.
Serves 1-2

Fillings for crêpes and omelettes soufflés

All these fillings will fill either 4 omelettes or 8 pancakes.

Abricot
Apricot
Make a sugar syrup with ½ cup + 2 tablespoons water and ½ cup sugar. Add 1 lb apricots, pitted, and poach gently until they are tender. When fresh apricots are not obtainable you can heat a 14-oz can of apricot halves. Blend 2 teaspoons arrowroot with 2 tablespoons of water and stir into the apricots. Bring to the boil, stirring all the time, and cook until thickened. If you like, you can add 2 tablespoons apricot brandy.

Citron à la crème
Lemon cream
Finely grate the rind of 1 large lemon and squeeze the juice. Whip 1¼ cups heavy cream until it just holds its shape, then fold in the lemon zest and juice and sweeten to taste with about ¼ cup superfine sugar.

Orange
Thinly peel the zest of 1 orange and cut into very fine strips. Cook in boiling water for 2 minutes, then drain, reserving the liquid. Peel 4 more oranges, removing all the white pith from all the oranges and cut into slices. Spoon 4 tablespoons of the reserved orange liquid into a saucepan with 4 tablespoons sugar, put over a low heat until the sugar has dissolved then boil rapidly until a golden caramel is reached. Cool slightly, add the orange slices and the prepared zest and cook over a gentle heat for a few minutes. If you like you can add 1-2 tablespoons of Cointreau.

Bananes au miel
Bananas with honey
Slice 3 bananas thinly, put into a bowl and sprinkle with a tablespoon of lemon juice. Heat 4 tablespoons of clear honey in

a saucepan, add the bananas and heat gently for a couple of minutes.

Framboises à la Lorraine
Raspberries

Sprinkle 12 oz-1 lb fresh raspberries with ¼ cup sugar and 2 tablespoons Framboise liqueur (or use Kirsch or Eau de Vie). Leave to stand for about 10 minutes. Lightly whip ⅔ cup heavy cream until it just holds its shape, then fold into the raspberies.

Ananas au Kirsch
Pineapple with Kirsch

Peel and remove the core of a small pineapple and chop into small pieces. Sprinkle with about a tablespoonful of sugar and 2 tablespoons Kirsch and leave for about 10 minutes.

Clafouti aux cerises de Limousin
Baked puffed cherry pancake

Clafoutis of various kinds are made all over France but the cherry one, which is made in Limousin during the summer, is one of the best-known. You can, however, use other fruit, such as apples, plums, prunes, or grapes, in the recipe below.

1 ½ lb cherries
⅓ cup superfine sugar
1 tablespoon brandy
2 cups sifted flour
pinch salt
3 eggs, separated
about 1 ½ cups milk
1 tablespoon butter

Pit the cherries, put into a buttered, shallow, ovenproof dish and sprinkle with 2 tablespoons of the sugar and the brandy. Combine the flour and salt in a bowl. Add the egg yolks and enough

milk to make a medium batter. Beat the egg whites until they form stiff peaks, then fold into the batter with the remaining sugar. Pour over the cherries and dot with the butter. Bake in a moderately hot oven (375°F) for about 40 minutes or until well risen and golden brown.
Serves 6

Pommes normande
Apples baked in cider

8 medium-sized cooking apples
4 tablespoons butter
⅓ cup brown sugar
1¼ cups medium dry cider

Peel and core the apples, but leave them whole and place in an ovenproof casserole. Blend the butter and sugar together and put a heaped teaspoonful in the centre of each apple. Pour over the cider, cover, and bake in a moderately hot oven (400°F) for about 45 minutes-1 hour. Baste the apples with the cider once or twice during cooking. Serve the apples warm with cream.
Serves 4

Poires au vin rouge
Pears in red wine

½ cup sugar
1¼ cups water
1 stick cinnamon or ¼ teaspoon ground cinnamon
2 tablespoons redcurrant jelly
8 small pears
1¼ cups red wine

Put the sugar, water, cinnamon and redcurrant jelly into a

saucepan and heat gently until the sugar and jelly have dissolved. Peel the pears, but leave them whole with the stems intact. Put the pears into the saucepan, cover and cook very gently for 15 minutes. Remove the lid, add the wine and cook uncovered for a further 15 minutes. If you have used pears which are not quite ripe you may have to cook them for slightly longer. Remove the pears carefully with a slotted spoon and place in a serving dish. Boil the liquid rapidly until it is reduced to a thin syrup. Strain over the pears and chill.
Serves 4

Variation: This recipe can also be used for peaches, which should not be quite ripe. Plunge them into boiling water for 1 minute, then refresh in cold water so that the peel can be easily removed. Cook for 10 minutes without the wine, then add the wine and cook for a further 10 minutes or until tender.

Poires agenaises
Pears with prunes

This makes a delicious, simple dessert for the winter when pears are generally fairly cheap.

½ lb prunes
1 ¼ cups wine—either red or white, or you could use cider.
juice 1 lemon
½ cup sugar
1 vanilla bean or use a few drops vanilla extract
1 lb small pears

Soak the prunes overnight, or for several hours, in the wine. Turn into a saucepan and bring slowly to the boil with the lemon juice, sugar and vanilla bean or extract. Peel, core and quarter the pears and add them to the pan just before the liquid boils. Lower the heat and simmer gently for about 30 minutes or until the prunes and pears are quite tender. Taste and add extra sugar

if necessary and remove the vanilla bean, if used. Either serve hot or allow to become cold and then chill. Serve with cream.
Serves 4-6

Pêches flambées
Peaches in brandy

1 ¼ cups water
½ cup sugar
1 vanilla bean
4 large peaches
4 tablespoons brandy

Put the water, sugar and vanilla bean into a saucepan, heat gently until the sugar has dissolved, then simmer for 5 minutes. Plunge the peaches into boiling water for 1 minute, drain, and rinse in cold water. Peel off the skins, cut the peaches in half, and remove the pits. Add the peaches to the sugar syrup and poach them gently for about 4 minutes or until just tender. Remove from the pan with a slotted spoon, place on a heated serving dish and keep warm. Remove the vanilla bean and boil the sugar syrup rapidly until it is reduced by about half. Pour this over the peaches. Heat the brandy in the saucepan, then pour over the peaches and ignite. Serve with cream.
Serves 4

Pommes au beurre
Buttered apples

These apples are delicious served hot on their own, but they also make a very good filling for an *omelette soufflé* (see page 213) and are also a traditional filling for pancakes (see page 212) in Brittany. If you are feeling extravagant, you can add 2 table-spoons Calvados at the end of the cooking.

2 lb cooking apples
¼ cup butter, preferably unsalted
¼ cup sugar

Peel, core and thinly slice the apples. Melt the butter in a large, shallow pan, then add the apples and the sugar. Cook gently until the apples are golden, then turn and cook them on the second side. Serve with cream.
Serves 4

Poires au chocolat
Pears with chocolate sauce

6 large pears
½ cup + 2 tablespoons water
¼ cup sugar
1 vanilla bean
4 oz unsweetened baking chocolate
2 tablespoons butter

Peel the pears, cut into quarters and remove the cores. Place in a pan with the water, sugar and vanilla bean and cook gently for about 10 minutes. Break the chocolate into a bowl over a pan of hot water and leave until melted, then stir in the butter and 2 tablespoons of the liquid from cooking the pears. Arrange the well-drained pears in an ovenproof dish and pour the melted chocolate over them. Cover and bake in a moderate oven (350°F) for 15 minutes. Serve with ice cream or cream.
Serves 4-6

Soufflé aux abricots
Apricot soufflé

I don't know if this can really be classified as a French recipe, but it is so simple that I felt it was worth including.

12-oz jar apricot jam
5 egg whites

Put the jam into a saucepan and heat gently until soft. Remove from the heat. Beat the egg whites until they form soft peaks, then fold them carefully into the jam mixture. Turn into a lightly buttered soufflé dish and bake in a moderately hot oven (400°F) for 25 minutes or until well risen and pale golden. Serve immediately with cream.
Serves 4-6

Soufflé aux pruneaux
Prune soufflé

A word of warning about this delicious soufflé — it is surprisingly rich so do not serve it at the end of an enormous meal.

½ lb prunes
¼ cup sugar
grated zest and juice 1 orange
½ cup + 2 tablespoons white wine
4 egg whites

Put the prunes to soak in cold water overnight. Drain and put into a saucepan with the sugar, orange zest and juice and white wine. Cover and simmer gently for about 1 hour or until the prunes are tender. Strain the prunes, reserving the juice, then either pit them and put into a blender with the juice, or sieve the mixture into the juice. Beat the egg whites until they are stiff

and form soft peaks, then carefully and quickly fold in the prune mixture. Turn into a well-buttered soufflé dish and bake in a moderately hot oven (375°F) for about 30 minutes.
Serves 6-8

Breads, pastries and gâteaux

There are very few French housewives who you will find make their own *brioches* and *croissants* — these, like a good many other items, are bought from the local *pâtisserie*. However, for the benefit of the enthusiastic I have included recipes for both of them as they are not very complicated to make. They freeze well and if you own a freezer I would always recommend making up a large batch and freezing some of them.

Pâte briseé

This is the French equivalent of our short crust pastry. In the recipes where I have referred to *pâte brisée* made with 1 cup of flour use ¼ cup butter and a small egg but omit the water unless the pastry is too dry: equally for pastry made with 1½ cups flour use ¼ cup + 2 tablespoons butter, 1 egg, and about 1 tablespoon of water.

2 cups flour
pinch salt
½ cup butter
1 egg
about 2 tablespoons water

Sift the flour and salt onto a working surface, which should preferably be a cold one, such as marble, although a formica working top is quite adequate. Cut the butter up into small cubes. Make a well in the centre of the flour and put in the butter, egg and water. Using your fingertips, work the butter, egg and water together with the flour until it is well blended. The dough should cling together, leaving the working surface clean, so you may have to add a little more water, but do not make it too wet. Knead the dough lightly for about 3 minutes until it forms a smooth ball, then put into a plastic bag and refrigerate for at least 30 minutes before using. The made-up dough can be stored in the refrigerator for a few days, but if it has been in the refrigerator for more than a few hours, it is advisable to remove it about 30 minutes before you wish to use it or it will be too hard to roll out. Use as required.

Pâte sucrée
Sweet short pastry

2 cups flour
pinch salt
½ cup butter
¼ cup superfine sugar
2 egg yolks

Sift the flour and salt onto a working surface. Cut the butter up into small cubes. Make a well in the centre of the flour and put in the butter, sugar and egg yolks. Using your fingertips, work the butter, egg and sugar together with the flour until it is all blended. The dough should cling together, leaving the working surface clean, so you may have to add a little water as well, but do not make it too soft. Knead the dough lightly for about 3 minutes until it forms a smooth ball, then put into a plastic bag and refrigerate for at least 30 minutes before using. The made-up dough can be stored in the refrigerator for a few days, but if it has been in the refrigerator for more than a few hours, it is advisable to remove it about 30 minutes before you wish to use it or it wil be too hard to roll out. Use as required.

Pâte à choux
Choux pastry

½ cup + 2 tablespoons flour
pinch salt
4 tablespoons butter
½ cup + 2 tablespoons water
2 eggs
1 egg yolk

Sift the flour and salt together. Put the butter, cut into small pieces, into a pan with the water. Put over a fairly gentle heat until the butter has melted, then bring to the boil. Remove the pan from the heat, add the flour all at once and beat well until the mixture forms a soft ball and leaves the sides of the pan clean. You may find it necessary to replace the pan over a very gentle heat, but do not allow it to cook after the flour has been added. Allow to cool down slightly, then beat in the whole eggs and the egg yolk, one at a time, until a very smooth, shiny mixture results. Use as required.

Pâte feuilletée
Puff pastry

There is no doubt that home-made puff pastry is delicious, but it is a great deal of bother to make and many of the commercially made packets of frozen pastry are excellent. If you do take a short cut and use these you must use double the amount of pastry given in a recipe, i.e. if a recipe states puff pastry made with 2 cups of flour, you must use a 14 oz-1 lb packet. Home-made puff pastry also freezes very well, so if you are going to the trouble of making it and you have a freezer, it is well worth making up a larger quantity.

2 cups flour
½ teaspoon salt

½ cup + 2 tablespoons water, preferably iced
1 teaspoon lemon juice
1 cup butter

Sift the flour and salt into a bowl. Add the water and lemon juice and mix to a soft dough. Soften the butter, then reform into an oblong. Roll the dough out to a rectangle 12 in x 8 in. Place the butter on top and fold the ends to the centre, like a parcel, to cover the butter. Press the centre edges and the sides to seal it. Give the pastry a half turn and roll it out again to a rectangle. Mark the dough into three and fold the lower third up and the top third down, like an envelope. Seal the edge. Put the dough into a plastic bag and leave to rest in the refrigerator for at least 20 minutes. Remove the dough from the bag, and roll and fold three times more before leaving it to rest again, then repeat this. The dough must be allowed to rest for an hour before using, after the final rolling and folding. Use as required.

Croissants

1 teaspoon sugar
1 cup warm water
1 tablespoon or 1 envelope dried yeast
4 cups flour
2 teaspoons salt
2 tablespoons lard
1 egg
¾ cup butter
For the egg wash:
1 egg
2 tablespoons water
½ teaspoon sugar

Dissolve the sugar in the water in a bowl and sprinkle the yeast over it. Leave for 10 minutes or until frothy. Sift together the flour and salt and rub in the lard. Beat the egg. Add the egg and yeast liquid to the flour and mix to a dough. Knead well.

Roll the dough out to a rectangle 20 in x 6 in. Divide the butter into three. Dot the top two-thirds of the dough with one part of the butter, leaving a clear band round the edge. Fold the dough in three by bringing up the plain part of the dough, then bringing the top part over. Turn the dough so that the fold is on the right-hand side. Seal the edges by pressing with the rolling pin. Re-shape the dough to a long rectangle by gently pressing at intervals with the rolling pin, taking care to keep a good shape. Repeat the above method twice, using the other two parts of the butter. Place the dough in an oiled plastic bag and allow to rest in a cold place or refrigerator for at least 30 minutes. Roll out as before to a rectangular strip. Repeat the folding and rolling three more times. Replace in the plastic bag and leave in a cold place or refrigerator for at least 1 hour. To shape the croissants, roll out the dough to a rectangle slightly larger than 18 in x 12 in, cover with oiled plastic wrap and leave for 10 minutes. Trim the edges with a sharp knife and divide in half lengthways. Cut each strip into 3 squares, then each square into 2 triangles.

For the egg wash, beat the egg with the water and sugar. Brush this over the triangles. Roll up each triangle loosely towards the point, finishing wih the tip underneath. Curve into a crescent. Brush the tops with egg wash and place on ungreased baking sheets. Cover with oiled plastic wrap and leave it to rise at room temperature for about 30 minutes until light and fluffy. Brush again with egg wash. Bake the *croissants* in a hot oven (425°F) for about 20 minutes or until golden brown.
Makes 12

Brioches

1 tablespoon sugar
1 ½ tablespoons warm water
2 teaspoons dried yeast

2 cups flour
½ teaspoon salt
4 tablespoons butter
2 eggs
To glaze:
1 egg

Dissolve ½ teaspoon of the sugar in the warm water. Sprinkle the dried yeast over it and leave for 10 minutes or until frothy. Sift together the flour and salt and add the remaining sugar. Melt the butter and allow it to cool. Beat the eggs. Add the yeast liquid, eggs and butter to the flour and work to a soft dough. Turn onto a lightly floured surface and knead for 5 minutes. Place the dough in an oiled plastic bag and leave to rise for 2-3 hours in a cool place.

Grease twelve 3-in brioche pans well. Turn the risen dough onto a floured surface and divide into twelve. Knead lightly and form three-quarters of each piece into a ball. Place in a pan and firmly press a hole in the centre. Roll the remaining quarter into a ball and place on top. Put the pans on a baking sheet and cover with oiled plastic wrap. Leave to rise at room temperature for about 1 hour or until light and puffy. Beat the egg for glazing and brush over the risen *brioches*. Bake in a very hot oven (450°F) for about 10 minutes or until well risen and golden brown. Serve warm.
Makes 12

Tarte aux demoiselles Tatin
Upside-down apple pie

4 tablespoons butter
⅓ cup brown sugar
2 lb cooking apples - these should be of a fairly firm type
pâte brisée or *sucrée* made with 1 cup flour (see pages 223, 224)

Melt the butter and brush just over half of it over the bottom and

sides of a deep cake pan 8-9 in. in diameter. Sprinkle with just over half the sugar. Peel, core and slice the apples and put into the cake pan. Sprinkle with the remainder of the butter and sugar. Roll out the pastry and cut out a circle the size of the cake pan. Place this on top. Bake the tart in a moderately hot oven (400°F) for about 45 minutes. Serve either warm, or cold with cream.
Serves 6

Tarte aux pommes normande
Apple tart

pâte sucrée made with 1 cup flour (see page 224)
2 lb cooking apples
3 tablespoons water
½ cup sugar
1 tablespoon lemon juice
2 tablespoons apricot jam

Roll out the pastry and use to line a flan ring or pan about 8-9 in. diameter. Peel, core and slice 1½ lb of the apples, put into a saucepan with the water and sugar and cook until soft. Mash with a fork to give a smooth purée, then spoon into the flan case. Peel and core the remaining apples and slice neatly. Arrange these in a circle on top of the apple purée and brush them with lemon juice. Bake in a moderately hot oven (375°F) for 25 minutes. Sieve the apricot jam into a saucepan and heat gently. Remove the flan from the oven and brush all over the top with the warm jam. Serve this tart either hot or cold.
Serves 4-6

Bourdelots normande
Stuffed apples in pastry

4 tablespoons butter
¼ cup raisins
grated zest of 1 orange
4 large eating apples
pâte sucrée made with 2 cups flour (see page 224)
1 egg yolk
2 tablespoons water

Lightly cream the butter, then work in the raisins and orange zest. Peel and core the apples, but leave them whole and stuff the centre of each apple with some of the butter mixture. Roll out the pastry and cut into 4 circles. Brush the edges with the egg yolk, beaten with the water. Wrap the pastry round the apples, making sure they are completely covered and sealed in, and place on a baking sheet with the seams underneath. Brush all over the pastry with the egg wash. Bake in a moderately hot oven (400°F) for 45 minutes. Serve warm with cream.
Serves 4

Tarte aux pêches
Peach tart

pâte brisée made with 1 cup flour (see page 223)
3 peaches or use a 14-oz can peach halves
2 eggs
2 tablespoons superfine sugar
1 cup milk
few drops vanilla extract
4 tablespoons cake crumbs

Roll out the pastry and use to line an 8-in. fluted flan ring or pan. If using fresh peaches, peel and halve them and remove the pits. If using canned peaches, drain well. Arrange the peach halves in the bottom of the flan case. Beat the eggs with the sugar,

milk and vanilla extract then add the cake crumbs. Pour this mixture over the peaches. Bake the flan in a moderate oven (350°F) for about 30 minutes. Serve warm.
Serves 4-6

Tarte aux abricots
Apricot tart

Although apricots are used here, they can be replaced with other fruit, e.g. peaches, strawberries, pitted cherries.

pâte sucrée made with 1 cup flour (see page 224)
1 ½ lb fresh apricots ⎤ or use 1 lb 14-oz can
1 ¼ cups water   ⎥ apricots
½ cup sugar   ⎦
1 ¼ cups *crème pâtissière* (see page 201)
2 teaspoons arrowroot

Roll out the pastry and use it to line a 9-in fluted flan ring. Fill the centre with buttered, lightweight foil and baking beans and bake in a moderately hot oven (400°F) for about 20 minutes. Remove the foil and beans and bake for a further 5-10 minutes to dry out the base. Remove from the oven and leave to cool.

Halve the fresh apricots and remove the pits. Heat the water and sugar in a saucepan over a gentle heat for about 5 minutes or until the sugar has dissolved. Add the apricots to the pan and poach them gently for about 5 minutes or until they are just tender. Allow to cool.

Either drain the freshly poached apricots from their juice or drain the canned apricots. Dry them well on paper towels. Spread the *crème pâtissière* over the base of the flan, then arrange the apricot halves on top. Measure the apricot syrup and blend ¾ cup of it with the arrowroot. Put into a small saucepan and bring to the boil, stirring all the time until thickened and clear. Allow to cool for a couple of minutes, then spoon this glaze over the fruit. Leave until set.
Serves 6-8

Poirat du Berry
Pear pie

2 lb pears
3 tablespoons brandy
¼ cup sugar
pâte brisée made with 1 cup flour (see page 223)
1 egg yolk
1 tablespoon water
½ cup + 2 tablespoons cream

Peel, core and slice the pears, put into a bowl and sprinkle with the brandy and sugar. Leave for about 1 hour. Using a slotted spoon, remove the pears from the brandy and sugar, and place in a pie dish. Roll out the pastry so that it is about 1 in. larger than the pie dish. Cut off a strip of pastry ½ in. wide and place round the rim of the dish. Beat the egg yolk with the water and brush over the pastry edge. Lay the rolled out pastry over the top of the pears. Seal the pastry edges and neaten them, then brush all over the top with the remainder of the egg wash. Make a hole about 1 in. in diameter in the centre of the pastry. Bake the pie in a moderately hot oven (375°F) for 30 minues. Blend the cream with the brandy left from soaking the pears and pour this through the hole in the top of the pie. Return to the oven for a further 5 minutes.
Serves 6

Gâteau Saint-Honoré

pâte sucrée made with 1 cup flour (see page 224)
pâte à choux made with 5 tablespoons flour (see page 225)
1 ¼ cups *crème Chantilly* (see page 202) or *crème pâtissière* (see page 201)
½ cup sugar
4 tablespoons water
fresh fruit to decorate

Roll out the *pâte sucrée* to a 7-in circle and place on a baking tray. Prick lightly all over with a fork and bake in a moderate oven (350°F) for about 15-20 minutes or until pale golden brown at the edges. Cool on a wire rack. Using either a piping bag and ½-in. plain nozzle, or two teaspoons, put small blobs of the *pâte à choux*, the size of a large grape, on a greased baking sheet. Bake in a moderately hot oven (400°F) for about 15 minutes or until golden. Cool on a wire rack. When cold, split the puffs almost in half and fill each one with about a teaspoon of the *crème Chantilly* or *crème pâtissière*. Put the sugar and water into a small, heavy saucepan and place over low heat until the sugar has dissolved, then boil rapidly until a pale golden colour. Quickly remove the pan from the heat. Holding the puffs on a fork, dip them into the caramel and arrange them round the edges of the pastry base. If the caramel begins to harden before you have coated all the puffs, replace it over a gentle heat. Spoon the remaining cream into the centre of the pastry base and decorate with fresh fruit.

Serves 8

Profiteroles
Choux pastries with chocolate sauce

pâte à choux made with ¼ cup + 2 tablespoons flour
(see page 225)
½ cup + 2 tablespoons *crème Chantilly* (see page 202)
6 oz unsweetened baking chocolate
½ cup + 2 tablespoons milk
1 egg yolk

Using either a piping bag with a ½-in plain nozzle or two teaspoons, put heaps of the *pâte à choux* the size of a plum, on two greased baking sheets. You should be able to make about 20 with this quantity of pastry and they should be spaced well apart to allow for rising. Bake in a moderately hot oven (400°F) for about 25 minutes or until golden brown. Remove the puffs from the oven and allow to cool.

Split the puffs almost in half and fill each one with about a teaspoon of cream. Pile them up on a serving dish and chill. Break the chocolate into small pieces and put into a bowl over a pan of hot water. Pour the milk into a saucepan, bring just to the boil and leave to cool for about 10 minutes, then beat in the egg yolk. When the chocolate has melted, gradually beat in the milk and egg mixture. Increase the heat in the pan below so that the water is just boiling and leave for about 5 minutes. Just before serving, pour the hot chocolate sauce over the puffs and serve as soon as possible.
Serves 6

Éclairs

pâte à choux made with ½ cup + 2 tablespoons flour
(see page 225)
1¼ cups *crème Chantilly* (see page 202)
6 oz unsweetened baking chocolate

Spoon the *pâte à choux* into a piping bag with a ½-in. plain nozzle and pipe out 3-in. lengths onto two greased baking sheets. You should be able to make about 18 with this quantity of pastry and they should be spaced well apart to allow for rising. Bake in a moderately hot oven (400°F) for about 25 minutes or until golden brown. Remove the *éclairs* from the oven and allow to cool.

Make a slit all the way along one side of each *éclair* and fill the piping bag with the *crème Chantilly*. Pipe about a teaspoonful of cream into each *éclair*. Break the chocolate into small pieces and put into a wide bowl over a pan of hot water. When melted remove from the heat and dip the top of each *éclair* into the chocolate until well coated. Leave on a wire rack until the chocolate has set.
Makes about 18

Tarte au fromage blanc
Cheesecake

This recipe comes from Alsace.

pâte brisée made with 1 cup flour (see page 223)
12 oz cream cheese
2 eggs, separated
½ cup sugar
4 tablespoons milk
½ cup flour
½ teaspoon vanilla extract
grated rind 1 small lemon
½ cup + 2 tablespoons heavy cream

Roll out the pastry thinly and use to line a 9-in. flan ring or pan.
Prick the base lightly with a fork. Sieve the cream cheese and beat
in the egg yolks, then the sugar, milk, flour, vanilla extract and
lemon rind. Mix well. Beat the egg whites until they form soft
peaks, then fold into the cheese mixture. Turn into the prepared
flan case and spread evenly. Bake in a moderate oven (350°F) for
1 hour. Allow to cool. Whip the cream until it just holds its shape
and spread over the top of the cheesecake. The cheesecake can be
decorated with fresh fruit if wished.
Serves 8

Savarin au rhum
Rum savarin

1 tablespoon lard
1 cup milk
1 teaspoon sugar
2½ teaspoons dried yeast
generous ½ cup butter
3 cups flour
pinch salt

3 eggs, beaten
2½ cups sugar
2½ cups water
8 tablespoons rum
2 lb fresh prepared fruit in season
To glaze:
3 tablespoons apricot jam
2 tablespoons water

Melt the lard and brush all over the bottom and sides of a 9-in. ring pan. Heat the milk to body temperature, then turn into a small bowl. Stir in the sugar and sprinkle in the dried yeast. Put into a warm place and leave for about 10 minutes or until the mixture is frothy. Melt the butter and leave it to cool. Sift the flour and salt into a large mixing bowl. Make a hollow in the flour, pour in the yeast mixture and beaten eggs and mix with a wooden spoon to a smooth dough. Using your hand, gradually mix in the butter. Continue to mix the dough for a few minutes by hand until it is really smooth. Turn into the greased pan, put into an oiled plastic bag and leave in a warm place for 30-40 minutes or until the dough has risen almost to the top of the pan. Take the pan out of the bag and bake the *savarin* in a hot oven (425°F) for about 25 minutes or until golden brown and firm. Leave to cool in the pan for 5 minutes, then turn out onto a rack with a deep plate underneath.

While the *savarin* is cooking, put the sugar into a saucepan with the water and place over low heat until the sugar has dissolved. Bring to the boil, then remove from the heat and stir in the rum. Using a fine skewer, make holes all over the warm *savarin*, then pour over the warm rum syrup. When all the syrup has been used, pour any which had drained onto the plate back into the pan. Pour over the *savarin* again. Repeat this until you have only about ½ cup of the syrup left. Place the *savarin* on a serving dish. Mix the reserved syrup with the prepared fruit and spoon this into the centre and round the outside of the *savarin*.

Melt the apricot jam in a pan with the water, strain, then brush this all over the outside of the *savarin*.
Serves 10

Gâteau aux noisettes d'Aubusson
Nut cake

This is a celebrated cake from the Limousin area.

1-1 ½ cups hazel nuts
⅓ cup clear honey
2 eggs
1 egg yolk
1 cup self-raising flour or all-purpose flour and 1 teaspoon baking powder, sifted
¼ cup superfine sugar
4 tablespoons softened butter

Scatter the nuts onto a tray and put into a moderate oven for about 10 minutes. Allow to cool, then rub them between your hands to remove the brown skins. Chop the nuts fairly finely.

In a mixing bowl, beat together the honey, eggs and egg yolk, the sifted flour and superfine sugar. Stir in the nuts and finally beat in the softened butter. Turn into a greased and lined shallow 8-in. cake pan and bake in a moderate oven (350°F) for 25-30 minutes. Allow to cool in the pan for a few minutes, then turn out onto a wire cooling rack. This cake is particularly good if the slices are thinly spread with butter.

Gâteau marbré
Marbled cake

6 tablespoons unsalted butter
4 eggs
½ cup superfine sugar

¾ cup flour, sifted
1 tablespoon cocoa
few drops vanilla extract

Melt the butter in a small saucepan, then put on one side to cool. Put the eggs into a large bowl with the sugar and place this over a pan of gently simmering water. Beat until the mixture is very thick and the whisk leaves a trail when lifted out. Remove the bowl from the heat and whisk for a further 2-3 minutes. Using a large, metal spoon, carefully fold in the butter and then all but a tablespoon of the sifted flour. Divide the cake mixture in half and carefully fold the cocoa into one half of the cake mixture. Fold a few drops of vanilla extract and the remaining sifted flour into the second half. Put heaped tablespoons of the chocolate and vanilla mixture alternately into a greased and floured 7-in cake pan. Bake in a moderate oven (350°F) for 50 minutes or until the top is golden brown and springs back when lightly pressed. Cool in the cake pan for a couple of minutes, then turn out onto a wire rack and leave to cool.

Gâteau au chocolat
Dark chocolate cake

¼ cup + 2 tablespoons self-raising flour
1 tablespoon cocoa
4 oz unsweetened baking chocolate
3 tablespoons water
½ cup butter
½ cup superfine sugar
4 eggs, separated
For the filling:
6 tablespoons apricot jam
2 tablespoons water
For the icing:
1 cup (confectioner's) sugar
1 tablespoon cocoa

2 oz unsweetened baking chocolate
4 tablespoons butter
2 tablespoons milk

Line an 8-in. round cake pan with oiled parchment paper. Sift together the flour and cocoa. Break the chocolate into small pieces and put with the water into a bowl over a pan of hot water; when melted remove from the heat and leave to cool.

Cream the butter and sugar together until light and fluffy. Beat the egg yolks in one at a time, beating well after each addition. Fold in the flour, alternately with the melted and cooled chocolate. Beat the egg whites until they form soft peaks, then fold carefully into the cake mixture. Turn into the prepared pan and bake in a moderate oven (350°F) for about 50 minutes or until a skewer inserted into the centre comes out clean. Remove the cake from the oven, leave for a few minutes, turn out onto a wire rack and leave to cool.

When the cake is cold, cut into three layers. Spoon the jam into a small saucepan with the water, bring to the boil, boil for 1 minute, then sieve. Brush the cut surfaces of the cake with some of the jam, reassemble the cake and brush the top and sides with the remainder.

Sift together the confectioner's sugar and cocoa. Break the chocolate into small pieces, put into a bowl with the butter and milk and place over a pan of hot water. Leave until the chocolate and butter have melted. Remove from the heat and beat in the sugar and cocoa until the icing is thick. Quickly spread the icing all over the cake and leave in a cool place to become firm.

Galette des rois
Three Kings cake

This cake is traditionally served on Twelfth Night. A 'lucky bean' or a tiny porcelain figure of a baby, which symbolizes the Christ child is inserted into the dough before baking and whoever finds this in his or her piece of cake becomes the king or queen of the evening. In northern France the *galette* is usually made with puff pastry, as in the recipe below, but in the south, *brioche* dough is more usual.

pâte feuilletée made with 2 cups flour (see page 225) or use a 14-oz. packet of frozen puff pastry, thawed
1 egg yolk
1 tablespoon water
1 ¼ cups *crème pâtissière* (see page 201)
2 tablespoons brandy

Roll out the pastry, cut into a circle about 8 in. in diameter and place on a baking sheet. Push a 'lucky bean' into the dough, then make an attractive pattern on top of the pastry using the sharp point of a knife. Blend the egg yolk with the water and brush this all over the top of the pastry. Bake in a very hot oven (450°F) for 10 minutes, then lower the heat to (400°F) for a further 10-15 minutes, or until the pastry is golden brown. Remove from the oven and allow to cool. Split the cake in half, spread the *crème pâtissière*, mixed with the brandy, over the bottom half, then replace the top half. The cake can be served cold, but it is nicer if you put it into a moderate oven (350°F) for about 10 minutes before you want to serve it so that it is just warm.
Serves 8

Gâteau Pithiviers
Almond cake

This cake is a specialty of Pithiviers which is a town just north of Orléans, but it can be found in *pâtisseries* all over France.

pâte feuilletée made with 2 cups flour (see page 225) or use a 14-oz. packet frozen puff pastry, thawed
⅔ cup blanched almonds
¼ cup + 2 tablespoons superfine sugar
4 tablespoons softened butter
2 teaspoons potato flour or cornstarch
2 egg yolks

1 tablespoon rum
To glaze:
1 egg, beaten
1 tablespoon confectioner's sugar

Make the pastry, roll out and cut into two rounds, one 8-in. and the other 9-in. in diameter. Place the smaller circle on a damp baking tray. Chop the almonds very finely — you can do this in a blender, but they should not be as fine as ground almonds. Mix the almonds with the sugar, butter, potato flour or cornstarch, eggs and rum. Blend well. Spread this mixture over the pastry on the baking sheet leaving ½-in. clear all round the border of the pastry. Brush this well with beaten egg and lay the second pastry circle on top. Seal the pastry edges well. With a sharp knife, make cuts in the top of the pastry to look like the spokes of a wheel. Brush all over with beaten egg and bake in a hot oven (425°F) for 25 minutes. Ten minutes before the end of cooking, remove the cake from the oven and dust the top with the confectioner's sugar. Return to the oven and leave so that the sugar caramelizes on the top.

This is delicious served either warm with cream for dessert, or cold, cut into slices, as a cake for tea.
Serves 6-8

Tuiles
Crisp almond cookies

2 egg whites
½ cup superfine sugar
½ cup flour, sifted
1 cup flaked almonds
4 tablespoons butter, melted
few drops almond extract

Lightly whisk the egg whites in a mixing bowl until they are frothy. Beat in the sugar and continue whisking until the sugar is well mixed in. Fold in the sifted flour, flaked almonds, butter and almond extract.

Put teaspoonfuls of the mixture onto greased trays, spacing them well apart to allow for spreading. Bake in a moderately hot oven (375°F) for about 6 minutes or until golden brown. Carefully lift the cookies off the tray with a spatula and place on greased rolling pins to cool; this gives the cookies a traditional curled shape. Store in an airtight tin until required.
Makes about 30

Colettes
Chocolate *petits fours*

These are not really a bread or pastry, but are so delicious that I had to include them somewhere! You will need about 18 waxed-paper candy cases which you should be able to buy in a gourmet equipment shop.

8 oz. unsweetened baking chocolate
4 tablespoons water
1 tablespoon strong coffee
4 tablespoons butter
2 egg yolks
1 teaspoon rum

Break 4 oz. of the chocolate into small pieces and put into a bowl over a pan of hot water. Leave until the chocolate has melted. Remove from the heat and put a good teaspoonful into each paper case. Using the handle of a teaspoon, spread the chocolate evenly round the base and sides of each case. Leave to set in a cool place.

Break the remaining chocolate into pieces and put into a small saucepan with the water and coffee. Put over low heat and, when the chocolate has melted, boil for 2 minutes, stirring frequently. Remove the pan from the heat and allow the mixture to cool.

Beat in the butter a little at a time, then blend in the egg yolks and rum. Leave in a cold place until thickened and completely cold. When the chocolate cases have set, peel off the paper cases very carefully. Spoon the filling into a piping bag with a ½-in. rose pipe and pipe the filling into each chocolate case, or use two teaspoons to spoon it in.

Makes 18

'Cigarettes'

These cookies are excellent served with ice-cream or mousse.

4 tablespoons butter
2 egg whites
½ cup superfine sugar
¼ cup + 2 tablespoons flour, sifted

Melt the butter, then leave to cool. Beat the egg whites until they form stiff peaks. Very carefully fold in the sugar, then the sifted flour and finally the butter; do this with the minimum amount of stirring. Put teaspoons of the mixture onto lightly greased baking trays and spread each thinly, to a 3-in. circle. Bake the cookies in a moderately hot oven (400°F).

When the cookies are golden round the edges, remove them one at a time from the baking trays with a sharp knife and wrap quickly round a pencil or thin wooden spoon handle. This must be done quickly or the cigarettes will harden and crack, so it is best to bake just a few at a time. Remove the cookies from the pencil or handle when firm, then leave to cool. Store in an airtight tin until required.

Makes about 30

Florentines

4 tablespoons butter
5 tablespoons sugar
2 tablespoons flour
⅓ cup blanched almonds, chopped
1 level tablespoon sultana raisins
1 level tablespoon mixed candied peel
3 glacé cherries, finely chopped
1 tablespoon heavy or light cream
2-3 oz. unsweetened baking chocolate

Melt the butter in a pan, add the sugar and boil for 1 minute.
Remove from the heat and blend in all the remaining ingredients
except the chocolate. Put teaspoons of the mixture onto greased
and floured baking trays, allowing plenty of space between each
one for the mixture to spread. Bake the florentines in a moderate
oven (350°F) for about 10 minutes or until they are golden
brown. Remove them from the oven and leave on the baking
trays for about 5 minutes, then place on a wire rack to cool. Melt
the chocolate in a bowl over hot water and, when the florentines
are cold, spoon a little melted chocolate over the flat side of each
cookie. Make a zig-zag pattern with a fork in the chocolate, then
put the cookies into a cold place until the chocolate has set. Store
in an airtight tin.
Makes about 15

Index

Aïoli, 16, 51
Almond cake, 240-41
Alouettes sans têtes, 138-9
Ananas au Kirsch, 215
Anchoïade, 58
Anchovy
  cheese and, omelette, 81
  paste, 58
Apple
  pie, upside-down, 228-9
  tart, 209
Apples
  baked in cider, 216
  buttered, 218-19
  stuffed, in pastry, 230
Apricot
  filling, 214
  soufflé, 220
  tart, 231
Artichoke soup, cream of,
  34
Artichokes with tomatoes, 194
Asparagus
  with hollandaise sauce, 189-90
  with melted butter, 190
  with sauce vinaigrette, 190
Asperges
  à la sauce hollandaise, 189-90
  au beurre, 190
  vinaigrette, 190

Ballottine de canard à l'orange,
  104-5
Bananes au miel, 214-15
Bavarois au chocolat, 207-8
Beef
  à la bourguignonne, 135
  and sausage pie, 141
  casseroled, 136-7
  fillet of, in puff pastry, 131-2
  in pot-au-feu, 138
  in red wine with olives, 134
  olives, 138-9
  pepper steak, 133
  salad, 57
  steaks with cream sauce, 132-3
  with vegetables and cider, 135-6
Beurre blanc, 14-15, 47
Black puddings, 15, 95
Blanquette de veau, 146-7
Boeuf
  à la bourguignonne, 18, 135
  à la mode, 136-7
  à la mode de Caen, 12, 135-6
  en daube, 134
Bouillabaisse, 16, 122-3
Bourdelots normande, 230
Brandade de morue, 17, 76, 109,
  111-12

Cabbage

partridge casseroled with, 186-7
red, with sausages, 165-6
rolls, 60
stuffed, 166-7
Cabillaud aux tomates, 113
Calvados (apple brandy), 12,
174-5, 218
Canapés au fromage, 87
Canard en gelée, 176
Caramel cream, 205-6
Carbonnade nîmoise, 155-6
Carottes
à la nivernaise, 194
potage froid aux, 42
Vichy, 193-4
Carré de veau au Chablis, 143
Carrots
glazed, 194
Vichy, 193-4
Carrot soup, iced, 42
Cassoulet 17, 164, 177
Cauliflower soup, 36-7
Caviar, 17
Celeriac soup, 29
Céléri rémoulade, 70
Celery
in *rémoulade* sauce, 70
potato, and endive salad, 67
Cèpes
à la crème, 193
farcis, 192
Champignons à la grecque, 61
Charcuterie, 14-15, 17, 55, 95
Cheese
and coffee cream, 211
and ham sandwich, 86
and leek soufflé, 83
and spinach soufflé, 82
Beaufort, 13
Bresse Bleu, 18
Brie, 9
cake, 235

Camembert, 12
choux pastry, 83-5
with leeks, 84-5
with spinach, 85
Coulommiers, 9
Emmenthal, 13, 20
fondue, 88
Fontainebleau, 9
Gournay, 12
Gruyère, 20
hearts, 202
Isigny, 12
Maroilles, 13
Neufchâtel, 12
omelette, 80
Parmesan, 20
Pont l'Évêque, 12
Reblochon, 13-14
Roquefort, 15
sauce, 46, 73, 87-8
Savoyard, 13-14
soufflé, 81-2
toasted, 87
Tomme, 13-14
Vacherin, 13
Cherry pudding, baked, 201,
215-16
Chestnut
mould, 209-11
soup, 31
Chicken
coq au vin, 18, 172
French roast, 169-70
fried, with cream sauce, 173-4
liver pâté, 96-7
pot-roast stuffed, 171
stuffed roast, with prunes, 170-
171
tarragon, 175-6
terrine, 99
with cider and apples, 174-5
with lemon, 169-70

with tomatoes and olives, 173
Chitterlings, 15, 95
Chocolate
  bavarois, 207-8
  cake, dark, 238-9
  chestnut soufflé, 210
  cream mould, 207-8
  petits fours, 242-3
  sauce, 219
  choux pastries with, 233-4
Chou
  farci à la provençale, 166-7
  rouge aux saucisses landais,
    165-6
  vert en paupiettes, 60
Choux
  pastries with chocolate sauce,
    233-4
  pastry, 225, 232, 233, 234
Cider, 12
  apples baked in, 216
  chicken with, and apples, 174-5
  dry, 131, 158, 182
  rabbit, 182
Cigarettes, 203, 243
Citron à la crème, 214
Citrons farcis aux sardines, 58-9
Clafouti aux cerises de Limousin,
    14, 201, 215-16
Cod with tomatoes, 113
Coeurs à la crème, 202
Cointreau, 214
Colettes, 242-3
Collier de mouton à la Bayonne,
    157-8
Concombres en salade, 69-70
Confectioners' custard, 201, 231,
    232, 233, 240
Confit d'oie, 17, 177
Consommé, 26-8, 137
Cookies
  chocolate *petits fours*, 242-3

cigarettes, 203, 243
  crisp almond, 241-2
  florentines, 244
Coquilles
  St-Jacques à la provençale, 124
  St-Michel, 123-4
Côtelettes d'agneau en cuirasses,
    156-7
Côtes de porc
  à la campagne, 162-3
  auvergnate, 161-2
  avesnoise, 161
  provençale, 163
Courgettes a la grecque, 61-2
Court bouillon, 47, 109-10
Crab
  salad, 56-7
  sea-bass stuffed with, 111
  soufflé, 83
  soup, cream of, 43-4
  with herbs and olives, 125
Crabe
  loup de mer farci au, 111
  niçoise, 125
  potage crème au, 43-4
  salade de, 56-7
  soufflé au, 83
Crème
  au moka, 203-4
  au vin blanc, 205
  de concombres, 39
  de coquillages, 42-3
  Dubarry, 36-7
  pâtissière, 201, 231-3, 240
  renversée, 205-6
  Saint-Valentin, 211
  tourangelle, 36
Crêpes, 212-15
Crisp almond cookies, 241-2
Croque monsieur, 86
Cucumber
  salad, 69-70

soup, cream of, 39

Desserts (cold)
apricot tart, 231
caramel cream, 205-6
cheese and coffee cream, 211
cheese hearts, 202
chestnut mould, 209-11
chocolate chestnut soufflé, 210
chocolate cream mould, 207-8
confectioners' custard, 201, 231,
    232, 233, 240
cream Chantilly, 202, 232, 233,
    234
floating islands, 206-7
fresh fruit, 201
macaroons with chocolate, 208
meringue cake with chestnuts,
    210-11
mocha cream, 203-4
peaches in red wine, 217
pears in red wine, 217
port wine jelly, 204
praline ice cream, 203
rum *bavarois*, 208
upside-down apple pie, 228-9
white wine cream, 205
Desserts (hot)
apples baked in cider, 216
apple tart, 229
apricot soufflé, 220
baked cherry pudding, 201, 215-
    216
bread dipped in egg and fried
    with cinnamon and sugar, 212
buttered apples, 218-19
pancakes, sweet, 212-15, 218
peaches in brandy, 218
peach tart, 230-31
pear pie, 232
pears with chocolate sauce, 219
pears with prunes, 217-18

prune soufflé, 220-21
soufflé omelette, 213-15, 218
stuffed apples in pastry, 230
Dindonneau farci aux marrons,
    179
Duck
in jelly, 176
stuffed, with orange, 104-5
terrine, 100

Eau de Vie, 215
Éclairs, 234
Egg and potato salad, 68
Eggplant, macaroni and, 190-191
Eggs
baked
    with cream, 77-8
    with pâté, 78
    with prawns, 78
Bénédictine, 76-7
hard-boiled
    stuffed, 74
    with garlic sauce, 74-5
    with ham, 75
    with haricot beans, 77
scrambled, with peppers and
    tomatoes, 78-9
soft-boiled, with herbs, 76
stuffed hard-boiled, 74
    with cheese sauce, 73-4
see also Omelettes
Épaule d'agneau aux noix, 155
Escalopes de veau à la savoyarde,
    142-3
Estouffade de pigeons, 185-6

Faisan en casserole, 185
Filet de boeuf en croûte, 131-2
Filet de porc normande, 160
Filets de merlan à la meunière,
    118
Filets de sole aux crevettes, 114

Fillings for soufflé omelettes
and sweet pancakes
apricot, 214
bananas with honey, 214-15
buttered apples, 218-19
lemon cream, 214
orange, 214
pineapple with Kirsch, 215
raspberries, 215
Fish, 109-30
Flageolet bean salad, 68-9
Flageolets, salade de, 68-9
Floating islands, 206-7
Florentines, 244
Foie d'agneau aux champignons,
159
Fonds
blanc, 26
brun, 26
de gibier, 27
de volaille, 27
Fondue savoyarde, 88
Framboise (liqueur) 13, 215
Framboises à la Lorraine, 215
French bean salad, 65
French dressing, *see Vinaigrette*
Fromage de tête, 105-6

Galantine
de boeuf et de jambon, 106-7
de veau, 107-8
Galantines
glazed beef and ham, 106-7
veal, 107-8
Galette
de pommes de terre, 196
des rois, 239-40
Garbure, 17, 30, 177
Garlic, 20
mayonnaise, 51
soup, 30-31

Gâteau
aux noisettes d'Aubusson, 237
de marrons, 209-11
marbré, 237-8
Pithiviers, 240-41
Gâteaux
almond cake, 240-41
cheesecake, 235
choux pastries with chocolate
sauce, 233-4
dark chocolate cake, 238-9
éclairs 234
marbled cake, 237-8
nut cake, 237
rum savarin, 235-7
Saint-Honoré, 232-3
Three kings cake, 239-40
Gelée au porto, 204
Gigot d'agneau
aux pommes Anna, 153
en croûte, 152-3
provençale, 153-4
Glace pralinée, 203
Goose
preserved, 177
with garlic and onions, 178
Gougère
aux épinards, 85
aux poireaux, 84-5
Green vegetable soup, 33
Grenadins de veau Corbigny, 145
Grey mullet
baked, 110
grilled, 111
Guinea fowl, braised, with
cream, 184
Ham omelette with herbs, 80
Hare
stuffed, with red wine sauce,
182-4
terrine, 100-101
Harengs à la nantaise, 121

Haricot bean
and tuna salad, 64-5
soup, 34-5
Haricot beans, Brittany-style,
191-2
Haricot de mouton, 158-9
Haricots blancs, salade de, 64-5
Haricots bretonne, 191-2
*Haricots verts, et d'oeufs, salade
de*, 65
Headcheese, 105-6
Herb omelette, 80
Herrings
Lyonnais, 120-21
with soft roe sauce, 121
Homard thermidor, 128
Hors d'oeuvres (cold)
anchovy paste, 58
cabbage rolls, 60
lemons stuffed with sardines,
58-9
mushrooms stewed in olive oil,
61
open tomato sandwich, 59
ratatouille, 61, 82
smoked trout mousse, 57-8
zucchini stewed in olive oil with
tomatoes, 61-2
Hors d'oeuvres (hot)
baked eggs with cream, 77-8
cheese choux pastry, 83-5
crab with herbs and olives, 125
eggs Bénédictine, 76
sardines
with spinach, 115-16
with tomatoes, 114-15
scallops Provencale, 124
scampi cooked with tomatoes,
124-5
soft-boiled eggs with herbs, 76

Ice cream, praline, 203

Iced carrot soup, 42
Îles flottantes, 206-7

Kirsch, 13, 215
Kugelhopf, 13

Lamb
and vegetable casserole, 157-8
cutlets in pastry cases, 156-7
kidneys with onions and
mushrooms, 159-60
leg of, Provençale, 153-4
liver, with mushrooms, 159
roast leg of
in pastry case, 152-3
with potatoes, 153
roast loin of, 151-2
shoulder of, stuffed with
walnuts, 155
sweetbreads, 149
with potatoes and carrots, 155-6
Langoustines provençale, 124-5
Langue de boeuf au gratin, 141-2
Lapin
à la campagne, 181
à la moutarde, 180
au cidre, 181-2
terrine de, 100-101
Leek and potato soup, chilled, 47
Leeks in French dressing, 69
Lemons stuffed with sardines,
58-9
Lentil
salad, 64
soup, 37
Lentilles de Puy, 14, 21
Lièvre
à la royale, 182-4
terrine de, 100-101
Lobster Thermidor, 128
Longe d'agneau à l'orléanaise
151-2

Loup de mer farci au crabe, 111

Macaroni à la languedocienne,
   190-91
Macaroni with eggplant, 190-
   191
Macaroons with chocolate, 208
Macédoine provençale, 66-7
Mackerel
   grilled, 110
   with prawns and shrimps, 116
Maquereaux à la bretonne, 116
Marbled cake, 237-8
Marrons glacés, 210-11
Mayonnaise, 45, 50, 51, 67, 68
Meat, 131-68
Mediterranean fish stew, 122-3
Merlans
   à la bretonne, 119-20
   au four, 119
Minestrone, 32
Mixed rice salad, 65-6
Mixed vegetable soup, 36
Mocha cream, 203-4
Morue brestoise, 112-13
Moules
   au gratin, 127
   marinière, 126-7
   salde de, 56
Mousse à la truite fumée, 57-8
Mushroom
   flan, 91-2
   omelette, 80
   soufflé, 83
Mushrooms, 21
   in cream, 193
   stewed in olive oil, 61
   stuffed, 192
Mussels
   marinière, 126-7
   salad, 56
   with garlic and breadcrumbs, 127

Nut cake, 237

Oeufs
durs
   à l'ail, 74-5
   à la bretonne, 77
   au jambon, 75
   farcis à la sauce Mornay, 73-4
   farcis provençale, 74
en cocotte
   à la crème, 77-8
   au pâté, 78
   aux crevettes, 78
   mollets fines herbes, 76
Oie à la poitevine, 178
Oignons au four, 198
Omelette
   au fromage, 80
   au jambon et aux fines herbes, 80
   aux anchois et au fromage, 81
   aux champignons, 80
   aux fines herbes, 80
   Parmentier, 80
   provençale, 81
Omelettes
   anchovy and cheese, 81
   cheese, 80
   ham, with herbs, 80
   herb, 80
   mushroom, 80
   potato, 80
   ratatouille, 81
Onion
   and potato soup, 37-8
   soup, 32
   tart, 89
Onions, oven-baked, 198

Pain perdu, 212
Pan bagna, 59
Pancake mixture, basic, 86, 212-
   213

Pancakes, sweet, 212-15, 218
Pannequets au jambon, 86
Partridge, casseroled, with
  cabbage, 186-7
Pastries
  apple tart, 229
  apricot tart, 231
  mushroom flan, 91-2
  onion tart, 89
  peach tart, 230-31
  pear pie, 232
  quiche Lorraine, 13, 73, 88-9
  spinach tart, 90
  stuffed apples in pastry, 230
  tomato and onion flan, 73, 90-91
  tomato flan, 92-3
  upside-down apple pie, 228-9
Pastry
  choux, 225, 232, 233, 234
  puff, 225, 240-41
  short crust, 223-4, 228, 230, 232,
    235
  sweet short, 224, 228, 229, 230,
    231, 232
Pâte
  à choux, 225, 232, 233, 234
  brisée, 223-4, 228, 230, 232, 235
  feuilletée, 225-6, 240
  sucrée, 224, 228, 229, 230, 231,
    232
Pâté
  aux pommes de terre, 195-6
  de campagne, 97-8
  de foie de volaille, 96-7
  de foie simple, 96
Pâté
  chicken liver, 96-7
  country-style, 97-8
  liver, simple, 96
  pork liver, Perigord style, 98-9
Paupiettes de veau, 144
Peaches

in brandy, 218
in red wine, 217
Peach tart, 230-31
Pear pie, 232
Pears
  in red wine, 216-17
  with chocolate sauce, 219
  with prunes, 217-18
Peas, French-style, 198-9
Pêches flambées, 218
Perche en papillotes, 117-18
Perch in a parcel, 117-18
Perdrix au chou, 186-7
Pesto, 32
Petit salé aux lentilles, 14, 165
Petits pois à la française, 198-9
Pheasant, casseroled, with port,
  185
Pigeon casserole, 185
Pig's kidneys in red wine, 167-8
Pike fish balls, 17-18, 129-30
Pintade en cocotte à la crème, 184
Pipérade, 17, 78-9
Pissaladière, 73, 90-91
Poirat du Berry, 232
Poireaux
  au jambon, sauce Mornay, 87-8
  vinaigrette, 69
Poires
  agenaises, 201, 217-18
  au chocolat, 219
  au vin rouge, 216-17
Poisson grillé au fenouil, 110
Poitrine de veau farcie aux olives,
  148
Pommes
  au beurre, 218-19
  Dauphine, 197
  normande, 216
Pommes de terre
  frites, 189
  lyonnaise, 197-8

Pork
and rabbit, potted, 103
chops
marinated, with herbs, 162-3
with cabbage and cheese, 161-162
with cheese, 161
with tomatoes, mushrooms and garlic, 163
kidneys, in red wine, 167-8
liver pate, Perigord-style, 98-9
potted, 102
salt
and haricot bean casserole, 164
with lentils, 165
tenderloin, with mushrooms, 160
Port wine jelly, 204
Potage
au potiron, 35-6
berrichon, 33
crème au crabe, 43-4
crème d'artichauts, 34
cressonnière, 40
froid aux carottes, 42
Parmentier, 37-8
Périgord, 28-9
Potato
and onion soup, 37-8
and tomato salad, 66-7
and watercress soup, 40
cake, 196
celery and endive salad, 67
omelette, 80
pie, 195-6
puffs, fried, 197
saute, with onions, 197-8
Pot-au-feu, 27, 137-8
Potted pork, 102
Potted pork and rabbit, 103
Poulet
à l'estragon, 175-6
au citron, 169-70

au riz à la campagne, 171
farci aux pruneaux, 170-71
niçoise, 173
roti à la française, 169-70
sauté à la crème, 173-4
Vallée d'Auge, 174-5
Poultry, 169-79
Praline ice cream, 203
Prawns
mackerel with, 116
sole with, 114
Profiteroles, 233-4
Prune soufflé, 220-21
Puff pastry, 225-6, 240-41
Pumpkin soup, 35-6
Purée aux épinards, 40-41

Quenelles de brochet, 17-18, 129-130
Queue de boeuf aux olives noires, 140
Quiche Lorraine, 73, 88-9

Rabbit
cider, 181-2
mustard, 180
potted pork and, 103
stew, 181
terrine, 100-101
Ratatouille, 22, 62, 81
Red mullet
grilled, 110
with mushrooms and herbs, 121-2
Red pepper salad, 63-4
Rice
and artichoke salad, 70-71
salad, mixed 65-6
Rillettes
de lapin, 103
de porc, 15, 102-3

Ris de veau
  à la crème et au jambon, 149
  aux herbes, 150
Rognons
  d'agneau à la mode de Bourges,
    159-60
  de porc au vin rouge, 167-8
  de veau aux raisins, 151
Romsteck à la crème, 132-3
Romsteck au poivre, 133
Rougets niçois, 121-2
Rum savarin, 235-7

Saint-Émilion au chocolat, 208
Salad dressings
  French, *see Vinaigrette*
  garlic mayonnaise, 51
  mayonnaise, 45, 50, 51, 67, 68
  vinaigrette, 45, 52-3, 57, 60-61,
    63, 64, 65, 67, 68, 69, 70, 190
Salade
  aux artichauts bretonne, 70-71
  cévenole, 67
  concombres en, 69
  de boeuf, 57
  de crabe, 56-7
  de flageolets, 68-9
  de haricots blancs, 64-5
  de haricots verts et d'oeufs, 65
  de lentilles, 64
  de moules, 56
  de piments, 63-4
  de riz, 65-6
  de tomates, 67
  d'oeufs et de pommes de terre,
    68
  niçoise, 16, 63
Salads
  beef, 57
  celery in *rémoulade* sauce, 70
  crab, 56-7
  cucumber, 69-70

egg and potato, 68
flageolet bean, 68-9
French bean, 65
haricot bean and tuna, 64-5
leeks in French dressing, 69
lentil, 64
mixed rice, 65-6
mussel, 56
potato and tomato, 66-7
potato, celery and endive, 67
red pepper, 63-4
rice and artichoke, 70-71
tomato, 67-8
tomato and egg, 60-61
Salt cod, 109
  creamed, 111-12
  with potatoes, 112-113
Salt meadow lamb,
  accompaniments to, 9, 190-91
Sardines
  aux épinards, 115-16
  citrons farcis aux, 58-9
  gratin de, aux tomates, 114-15
Sardines
  lemons stuffed with, 58-9
  with spinach, 115-16
  with tomatoes, 114-15
Sauces
  béchamel, 36-7, 45, 46, 74, 91-2,
    96
  Bercy, 46-7
  bigarade, 49-50
  butter and shallot, 47
  Chablis, 143
  cheese, 46, 73, 87-8
  chocolate, 219
  cream, 132-3, 145, 173
  espagnole, 45, 48
  Genoese, *see Pesto*
  gribiche, 52
  herb and caper, 52
  hollandaise, 53, 76-7, 189-90

Mornay, 46, 73, 87
orange, 49-50
pesto, 32-3
red wine, 183-4
rémoulade, 51-2, 70
rich brown, 45, 48
shallot and white wine, 46-7
shrimp, 129-30
soft roe, 121
tomato, 48-9
wine, 141-2
Sauté de veau chasseur, 146
Savoury flans and tarts
mushroom, 91-2
onion, 89
quiche Lorraine, 73, 88-9
spinach, 90
tomato, 92-3
tomato and onion, 73, 90-91
Savoury stuffed pancakes with
ham, 86
Scallops
with cheese and cream, 123-4
with garlic butter, 124
Scampi cooked in tomatoes, 124-
125
Sea-bass
baked, 111
grilled, 109-10
stuffed with crab, 111
Sea-bream
baked, 111
grilled, 110
Shellfish, 122-128
Short crust pastry, 223-4, 228,
230, 232, 235
Shrimps, mackerel with, 116
Shrimp sauce, 129-30
Smoked trout mousse, 57-8
Sole with prawns, 114
Soufflé
au chocolat et aux marrons, 210

au crabe, 83
au fromage, 81-2
au fromage et au jambon, 83
au fromage et aux épinards, 82
au fromage et aux poireaux, 82
aux abricots, 230
aux champignons, 83
aux pruneaux, 220-21
Soufflés
apricot, 220
cheese, 81-2
cheese and ham, 83
cheese and leek, 82
cheese and spinach, 82
chocolate chestnut, 210
crab, 83
mushroom, 83
prune, 220-21
Soupe
à l'ail, 30-31
à la bretonne, 34-5
à la savoyarde, 29
à l'oignon, 32
au pistou, 32-3
aux marrons, 31
Soups
aspic jelly, 26, 28, 106-7
carrot, iced, 42
cauliflower, 36-7
celeriac, 29
chestnut, 31
consommé, 26-8, 137
cream of artichoke, 34
cream of crab, 43-4
cream of cucumber, 39
cream of shellfish, 42-3
fresh tomato, 38-9
garbure, 17, 30, 177
garlic, 30-31
green vegetable, 33
haricot bean, 34-5
iced carrot, 42

Soups *continued*
leek and potato, chilled, 41
lentil, 37
mixed vegetable, 36
onion, 32
Périgord, 28-9
potato and onion, 37-8
potato and watercress, 40
pumpkin, 35-6
spinach, 40-41
vegetable, with pesto sauce, 32-3
Vichyssoise, 41
Spinach
soup, 40-41
tart, 90
Steaks with cream sauce, 132-3
Stock, 25-7
Sweet short pastry, 224, 228, 229
230, 231, 232

Tarte
à l'oignon, 89
au fromage blanc, 235
aux abricots, 231
aux champignons, 91-2
aux demoiselles Tatin, 228-9
aux épinards, 90
aux pêches, 230-31
aux pommes normande, 229
Terrine
de canard, 100
de lapin, 100-101
de lièvre, 100-101
de porc, 101-2
de poulet au citron, 99
Terrines
chicken with lemon, 99
duck, 100
hare, 100-101
headcheese, 105-6
pork, 101-2
potted pork, 102-3

potted pork and rabbit, 103
rabbit, 100-101
stuffed duck with orange, 104-5
Three Kings cake, 239-40
Tomates accordéon, 60-61
Tomato
and egg salad, 60-61
and onion flan, 73, 90-91
flan, 92-3
salad, 67-8
soup, fresh, 38-9
Topinambours aux tomates, 194-5
Tourte morvandelle, 141
Trout
in a parcel, 117-18
with almonds, 117
Truffat, 195-6
Truite
aux amandes, 117
en papillotes, 117-18
Tuiles, 241-2

Upside-down apple pie, 228-9

Vacherin aux marrons, 210-11
Veal
birds, 144
casserole, 146-7
escalopes with vermouth, 142-3
in cream sauce, 145
in puff pastry, 132
kidneys with grapes, 151
roast, with Chablis sauce, 143
stuffed breast of, with olives,
148
sweetbreads with cream and
ham, 149
sweetbreads with herbs, 150
with tomatoes and mushrooms,
146
Vegetables, 189-99
Vichyssoise, 41

Vinaigrette, sauce, 42, 52-3, 57,
60-61, 63, 64, 65, 67, 68, 69,
70, 190

White wine cream, 205
Whiting,
fillets *meunière*, 118

fish balls, 129-30
oven-baked, 119
with vegetables, 119-20
Wines, 13, 15, 17, 142, 143, 172

Zucchini stewed in olive oil with
tomatoes, 61-2